EMOTIONAL EATING

DROP THAT SPOON!

How To Maintain Emotional Self-Regulation and Rewire Your Brain Without The Need To Seek Comfort From Harmful Binge Eating Behaviors.

JAMES PERRY

Copyright © 2020 James Perry

All Rights Reserved

Copyright 2020 By James Perry - All rights reserved.

The following book is produced below with the goal of providing information that is as accurate and reliable as possible. Regardless, purchasing this eBook can be seen as consent to the fact that both the publisher and the author of this book are in no way experts on the topics discussed within and that any recommendations or suggestions that are made herein are for entertainment purposes only. Professionals should be consulted as needed prior to undertaking any of the action endorsed herein.

This declaration is deemed fair and valid by both the American Bar Association and the Committee of Publishers Association and is legally binding throughout the United States.

Furthermore, the transmission, duplication or reproduction of any of the following work including specific information will be considered an illegal act irrespective of if it is done electronically or in print. This extends to creating a secondary or tertiary copy of the work or a recorded copy and is only allowed with express written consent from the Publisher. All additional right reserved.

The information in the following pages is broadly considered to be a truthful and accurate account of facts and as such any inattention, use or misuse of the information in question by the reader will render any resulting actions solely under their purview. There are no scenarios in which the publisher or the original author of this work can be in any fashion deemed liable for any hardship or damages that may befall them after undertaking information described herein.

Additionally, the information in the following pages is intended only for informational purposes and should thus be thought of as universal. As befitting its nature, it is presented without assurance regarding its prolonged validity or interim quality. Trademarks that are mentioned are done without written consent and can in no way be considered an endorsement from the trademark holder.

Table of Contents

Introduction 13

    What Is Emotional Eating? 13

    What Is Binge Eating? 14

    What Is Bulimia? 14

PART I 15

Chapter 1: Understanding Your Food-Related Disorder 16

    Why Do People Eat Emotionally? 16

    Why Do People Binge Eat? 16

    Scientific Research on Eating Disorders and Why They Exist 17

    Why Do People Have Bulimia or Other Food Disorders? 18

    The Neuroscience of Brain Chemicals and Food As a Reward 19

Chapter 2: Understanding Your Mind 21

    Psychological and Emotional Triggers 21

    Childhood Causes 21

    Covering Up Emotions 22

    Feeling Empty or Bored 22

    Affection Deficiency 23

    Low Self-Esteem 23

    Mood 25

    Depression 25

    Anxiety 25

    Stress 26

Chapter 3: How to Stop Binge Eating, Bulimia, and Emotional Eating

....28

    Addressing the Core Wounds 28

    What Are Core Wounds? 28

    How to Address Them 29

    Positive Self-Talk 30

    What Is Positive Self-Talk? 31

    How to Use Positive Self-Talk? 32

Chapter 4: Making Healthier Decisions Using Intuitive 34

Eating 34

    Making Good Choices 34

    How to Begin Making Good Choices Using Intuitive Eating 34

    What Is Intuitive Eating? 35

    Intuitive Eating and Hunger 35

    The Benefits of Intuitive Eating 36

Chapter 5: Intuitive Eating Part 2 40

    How to Make Intuitive Eating Part of Your Life 40

    What Kind of Foods Should You Choose? 41

    Nutrients You Need and How to Get Them 45

    Magnesium 46

    Calcium 46

Chapter 6: How to Make These New Choices a Habit 46

    Healthy Thinking Patterns 47

    Healthy Lifestyle Changes 50

    30-Day Meal Plan 52

    Feta, mushroom and spinach, omelet. 52

    Oven-baked tempeh with broccoli and cauliflower rice...................... 52

    Chicken Caesar salad- tofu and romaine lettuce, parmesan................ 52

Chapter 7: What to Do Next 68

    How To Seek Help If It Becomes Uncontrollable? 68

    Counseling or Therapy 69

PART II..71

    Chapter 1: How to Reset Your Body?... 72

    Chapter 2: Science Behind Metabolism Reset....................................... 75

    Chapter 3: Recipes for Smoothies and Salads 77

        Green Smoothie... 77

        Strawberry Banana Smoothie.. 79

        Salmon Citrus Salad... 81

    Chapter 4: Quick and Easy Breakfast and Main Course Recipes 84

        Quinoa Salad.. 84

        Herb and Goat Cheese Omelet 87

        Mediterranean Cod.. 90

        Grilled Chicken and Veggies 92

        Stuffed Peppers 95

        Brussels Sprouts With Honey Mustard Chicken 99

        Quinoa Stuffed Chicken... 102

        Kale and Sweet Potato Frittata 105

        Walnut, Ginger, and Pineapple Oatmeal.. 107

        One-Pot Chicken Soup... 111

        Chocolate Pomegranate Truffles 113

Chapter 1: Anxiety, The Monster Within 116

    How Anxiety Overshadows Everyday Lives.. 118

What is Anxiety?... 118

Causes of Anxiety.. 118

Signs & Symptoms of Anxiety Disorders 119

Understanding Social Anxiety... 120

Symptoms of Social Anxiety 120

Chapter 2: Acknowledging Your Anxiety............................... 123

Common Anxiety Triggers 123

Getting to the Root Causes of Your Anxiety........................ 124

Negative Self-Talk 124

Unrealistic Expectations... 124

The "Should" Thoughts 125

Taking Things Too Personally 125

Pinpointing Your Anxiety.. 125

Chapter 3: Trauma and Anxiety... 128

Childhood Trauma and Sensitivity to Anxiety 129

Common Anxiety Disorders Caused by Trauma 129

Chapter 4: Grabbing your life back from anxiety................... 130

Managing Your Emotions 130

Don't react right away 130

Find healthy outlets 130

Look at the bigger picture 131

Replace your thoughts 131

Forgive your triggers.. 131

Using the Power of Mini Habits... 131

What Are Mini Habits?.. 132

What is *More* Essential than Your *Habits*?......................... 132

Benefits of Mini Habits.. 133

Chapter 5: Belittle anxiety with personal empowerment 134

Smile.. 134

Focus on solutions, not problems... 134

Notice the rise, not just the downfall 135

Just breathe 135

Fend off other's negativity 135

Switch the *"I have to"* mindset with *"I get to"* 135

Describe your life positively 136

Master rejection 136

Rethink challenges 137

Write in a gratitude journal.. 137

Chapter 6: Everyday techniques to fend off anxiety 138

Visualization and Anxiety 138

Why You Should Be Using Visualization....................................... 138

Aspects of Successful Visualization Practices................................ 142

Forms of Visualization for Anxiety 143

Meditation.. 143

Altered Memory Visualization.. 143

Receptive Visualization 144

Treasure Map 144

How to Design Your Own "Safe Space"... 145

Developing Anxiety Routines 147

Routines to Decrease Anxiety 148

The Importance of a Balanced Morning Routine 149

Benefits of a Morning Routine 149

Steps to Include in Your Morning Routine 149

Other Morning Methods to Relieve Anxiety 151

Chapter 7: Transforming Your anxiety for a better life 152

Using Anxiety to Your Advantage 152

Redefining danger 152

Channel your stress properly 153

Stop trying to do your best 153

Chapter 8: Battling anxiety like a true warrior 154

Spend time preparing 154

Learn to *manage* fear 154

Breathe 154

Don't keep things bottled up 156

Overpower that inner nagging voice 156

Think of the worst-case scenario 157

Reframe your mindset 157

Neuroplasticity 157

Get moving 158

Chapter 9: Rediscovering yourself after hurricane anxiety 160

When were you the *happiest*? 160

What makes you *unhappy*? 160

Write! 160

Learning to Love Yourself Again 161

Care about yourself as much as you care about others 161

Maintain boundaries 161

Do YOU? 162

Chapter 1: What is CBT? 165

The Science Behind It 165
How it Works 168
Changes Thought Patterns and Belief Systems 170
Its Purpose – Who it Can Help 171
How it Works on Anxiety and Depression....................................... 172
Depressive Disorders 177
How CBT Helps With Substance Abuse 179

Chapter 2: How CBT Can Help With… 182

Problem-Solving With Depression or Anxiety 183
CBT with Sleep Disorders 184

Chapter 3: Common Causes of Mood Disorders 186

Chemical Imbalances 187

Chapter 4: Understanding Your Moods and the Way You Think 191

How to Diagnose Your Negative Thought Patterns 192
Intrusive Thoughts 195
Examples of Some Intrusive Thoughts 196
Identifying Your Triggers for Anxiety and Stress 197

Chapter 5: How it Treats Mood Disorders 202

Practical Applications of CBT... 202
Setting Goals.. 204
Building Self-Esteem 205
Verbal Self-Talk.. 207
Counter Negative and Angry Feelings... 208
Dealing With Feelings of Guilt 208
Counteract Hopelessness... 209

Chapter 6: Steps to Dealing with Mood Disorders and Depression ... 210

Chapter 7: Multimodal Model 213
The Seven Modalities You Should Know About 214
Chapter 8: Rational Emotive Behavioral Therapy 217
A: Activating Event 217
B: The Belief 218
C: Consequences 218
D: Dispute 218
E: Effect 218
Chapter 9: Dialectical Behavior Therapy 219
Conclusion 222

Introduction

Be gentle with yourself throughout this process as it will be uncomfortable at times and will require strength. This book will help you through it, as you are not alone. I hope that this book also reminds you that many other people are suffering from the same type of food-related disorders as you are and that you are not alone in that either. This book will take a step-by-step approach, which will make for the highest chance of recovery. If at any time you need to take a break in order to think about the information you have learned, feel free to do so, but make sure you come back to this book quite soon after. Going through this process of recovery can be a lot, but with the right support, it will be possible.

You have already taken the first step in recovery, which is acknowledging that you have an issue. For that, I congratulate you!

What Is Emotional Eating?

Emotional eating occurs when a person suffering from emotional deficiencies of some sort, including lack of affection, lack of connection, or other factors like stress, depression, anxiety, or even general negative feelings like sadness or anger, eats in order to gain comfort from the food they are eating.

Many people find comfort in food. When people experience negative feelings and turn to food consumption in order to reduce their pain or to feel better, this is called emotional eating.

Now, some people do this on occasion like after a breakup or after a bad fight, but when this occurs at least a few times a week, this is when it is considered to have a negative impact on one's life and is when it becomes an issue that needs to be addressed.

What Is Binge Eating?

Binge eating disorder is another disorder that can be seen along with emotional eating. Binge eating disorder is when a person eats much more than a regular amount of food in a single occasion or sitting, and they feel unable to control themselves or to stop themselves. This could also be defined as a compulsion to overeat. In order to be considered a disorder, it has to happen at least two times per week for longer than six months consecutively.

Along with binge eating is overeating, although this is also sometimes seen as a separate disorder altogether. Overeating is when a person eats more than they require in order to sustain life. This occurs when they consume much more than they need in a day, or in a single sitting.

Overeating does not necessarily become binge eating, but it certainly can. Overeating is a general term used to describe the eating disorders that we just defined-Emotional Eating and Binge Eating. Thus, overeating could involve binge eating, food addiction, or other food-related disorders.

In this book, we will be focusing on emotional eating and binge eating, and how you can overcome these two food-related disorders.

What Is Bulimia?

Bulimia is another eating disorder. Bulimia involves binge eating, followed by extreme feelings of shame, guilt, and disdain for oneself and one's body. This is accompanied by intense feelings of body dysmorphia and body image issues, as well as the desire to be "skinnier." Thus, the person will turn to purging- or self-inflicted vomiting in an effort to lose weight and rid themselves of the guilt and shame.

PART I

Chapter 1: Understanding Your Food-Related Disorder

In this chapter, we are going to look at these two food-related disorders (binge eating/ bulimia and emotional eating) in much more detail. We will begin by looking at the most common reasons why people suffer from these disorders and will spend some time examining scientific research about why these disorders exist.

Why Do People Eat Emotionally?

The reason that emotional eating occurs is that eating foods that we enjoy makes us feel rewarded on an emotional and physiological level within our brain.

Why Do People Binge Eat?

People binge eat for a very similar reason to the reason why people experience emotional eating. This is because eating foods that we enjoy in terms of taste, smell, texture, and so on, makes us feel rewarded on an emotional and physiological level within our brains.

Throughout the rest of this chapter, we will look more in-depth at these eating disorders in order to give you more information about why they occur and what could cause them.

Scientific Research on Eating Disorders and Why They Exist

You may be asking how food cravings can result from emotional deficiencies and how these two seemingly unrelated things can be considered related. While we have touched on this briefly in this book already, the reason for this is that your body learns, over time, that eating certain foods makes it feel rewarding, positive, and happy for some time after it is ingested. These foods include convenience foods such as those containing processed sugars or salts, fast food, and quick pastries.

When you are sad or worried, your body feels negative and looks for ways to remedy this. Your brain then connects these two facts- that the body does not feel positive and that it wants to find a way to fix this. The brain then decides that eating the foods that make it feel good will remedy the situation. This process happens in the background of your mind without you being aware of it, and it leads you to consciously feel a craving for those specific foods such as sugary snacks or salty fast-food meals. You may not even be aware of why. If you then decide to give in to this craving and eat something like a microwave pizza snack, your body will feel rewarded and happy for a brief period of time. This reinforces to your brain that turning to food in an effort to make yourself feel better emotionally has been successful.

If you end up feeling down and guilty that you ate something that was unhealthy or that you ate too much, your brain will again try and remedy these negative emotions by craving food. This is how a cycle of emotional eating or a cycle of bingeing and purging can begin and continue. This could happen largely in your subconscious without you being any the wiser.

Why Do People Have Bulimia or Other Food Disorders?

Because scientists and psychiatrists understand this process that occurs in the brain, they know that food cravings can indicate emotional deficiencies. While there are other types of cravings that can occur, such as those that pregnant ladies experience, or those that indicate nutrient deficiencies, there are ways to tell that a craving is caused by some type of emotional deficiency.

It begins by determining the foods that a person craves and when they crave them. If every time someone has a stressful situation, they feel like eating a pizza, or if a person who is depressed tends to eat a lot of chocolate, this could indicate emotional eating. As you know by now, emotional eating and bulimia are closely related, and emotional eating can lead to bulimia over time.

If you crave fruit like a watermelon on a hot day, you are likely just dehydrated, and your body is trying to get water from a water-filled fruit that it knows will make it more hydrated. Examining situations like this has led scientists and psychiatrists to explore eating disorders in more depth and determine what types of emotional deficiencies can manifest themselves through food cravings or disordered eating in this way.

In the next chapter, we will look at psychological triggers that can lead to disordered eating.

The Neuroscience of Brain Chemicals and Food As a Reward

Many times, we may see ingredients on the packages of foods we eat, but we aren't really sure of exactly what they are, just that they taste good. In this section, we will take a deeper look at them and what they do to your brain.

Casein is a heavily processed ingredient that is derived from milk. It is processed a few times over and eventually creates milk solids that are concentrated. These milk solids- called Casein are then added into foods like cheese, french fries, milkshakes, and other fast and convenient packaged or fast-foods that contain dairy or dairy products (such as pastries and salad dressings). Casein has been compared to nicotine in its addictive properties. It is often seen in cheese, and this is why there is increasing evidence that people can become, and many are already addicted to cheese. The reason for this is during digestion. When cheese and other foods that contain casein are digested, it is broken down, and one of the compounds that it breaks down into is a compound that is strikingly similar to opioids- the highly addictive substance that is in pain killers.

High fructose corn syrup is surely an ingredient you have heard of before or at least one that you have seen on the packaging of your favorite snacks or quick foods. While this is actually derived from real corn, after it is finished being processed, there is nothing corn-like about it. High fructose corn syrup is essentially the same thing as refined sugar when all is said and done. It is used as a sweetener in foods like soda, cereal, and other sweet and quick foods. The reason why this ingredient is seen so often is that it is much cheaper than using sugar and is much easier to work with. High Fructose Corn Syrup is another common food additive that has been shown to be highly addictive. This substance has been shown to be similar to cocaine in its addictive properties.

MSG stands for Monosodium Glutamate, which sounds a lot like a chemical you may have encountered in science class in college. MSG is added to foods to give it a delicious flavor. It is essentially a very concentrated form of salt. What this does in foods such as fast-food, packaged convenience foods, and buffet-style food is that it gives it that wonderfully salty and fatty flavor that makes us keep coming back for more. Companies put this in food because it comes at an extremely low cost, and the flavor it brings covers up the artificial flavors of all of the other cheap ingredients that are used to make these foods. MSG has been known to block our natural appetite suppressant, which normally kicks in when we have had enough to eat. For this reason, when we are eating foods containing MSG, we do not recognize when we are satiated, and we continue to eat until we are stuffed because it tastes so great.

Chapter 2: Understanding Your Mind

In this chapter, we are going to look at some of the psychological factors that can lead to disordered eating so that you can gain a better understanding of what could have led you to use food as a means of coping.

Psychological and Emotional Triggers

There are several types of emotional deficiencies that can be indicated by disordered eating. We will explore these in detail below in hopes that you will recognize some of the reasons why you may be struggling with an eating disorder.

Childhood Causes

The first example of an emotional deficiency that we will examine is more of an umbrella for various emotional deficiencies. This umbrella term is Childhood Causes. If you think back on your childhood, think about how your relationship with food was cultivated. Maybe you were taught that when you behaved, you received food as a reward. Maybe when you were feeling down, you were given food to cheer you up. Maybe you turned to food when you were experiencing negative things in your childhood. Any of these could cause someone to suffer from emotional eating in their adulthood, as it had become something learned. This type is quite difficult to break as it has likely been a habit for many, many years, but it is possible. When we are children, we learn habits and make associations without knowing it that we often carry into our later lives. While this is no fault of yours, recognizing it as a potential issue is important to make changes.

Covering Up Emotions

Another emotional deficiency that can manifest itself in emotional eating and food cravings is actually the effort to cover up our emotions. Sometimes we would rather distract ourselves and cover up our emotions than to feel them or to face them head-on. In this case, our brain may make us feel hungry in an effort to distract us from the act of eating food. When we have a quiet minute where these feelings or thoughts would pop into our minds, we can cover them up by deciding to prepare food and eat and convince ourselves that we are "too busy" to acknowledge our feelings because we have to deal with our hunger. The fact that it is hunger that arises in this scenario makes it very difficult to ignore and very easy to deem as a necessary distraction since, after all, we do need to eat in order to survive. This can be a problem though, if we are not in need of nourishment, and we are telling ourselves that this is the reason why we cannot deal with our demons or our emotions. If there is something that you think you may be avoiding dealing with or thinking about or if you tend to be very uncomfortable with feelings of unrest, you may be experiencing this type of emotional eating.

Feeling Empty or Bored

When we feel bored, we often decide to eat or decide that we are hungry. This occupies our mind and our time and makes us feel less bored and even feel positive and happy. We also may eat when we are feeling empty. When we feel empty the food will quite literally be ingested in an effort to fill a void, but as we know, the food will not fill a void that is emotional in sort, and this will lead to an unhealthy cycle of trying to fill ourselves emotionally with something that will never actually work. This will lead us to become disappointed every time and continue trying to fill this void with material things like food or purchases. This can also be a general feeling of dissatisfaction with life and feelings of lacking something in your life. Looking deeper into this the next time you feel those cravings will be difficult but will help you greatly in the long term as you will then be able to identify the source of your feelings of emptiness and begin to fill these voids in ways that will be much more effective.

Affection Deficiency

Another emotional deficiency that could manifest itself as food cravings is an affection deficiency. This type of deficiency can be feelings of loneliness, feelings of a lack of love, or feelings of being undesired. If a person has been without an intimate relationship or has recently gone through a breakup, or if a person has not experienced physical intimacy in quite some time, they may be experiencing an affection deficiency. This type of emotional deficiency will often manifest itself in food cravings as we will try to gain feelings of comfort and positivity from the good tasting, drug-like (as we talked about in chapter one) foods they crave.

Low Self-Esteem

Another emotional deficiency that may be indicated by food cravings is a low level of self-esteem. Low self-esteem can cause people to feel down, unlovable, inadequate, and overall negative and sad. This can make a person feel like eating foods they enjoy will make them feel better, even if only for a few moments. Low self-esteem is an emotional deficiency that is difficult to deal with as it affects every area of a person's life, such as their love life, their social life, their career life, and so on. Sometimes people have reported feeling like food was something that was always there for them, and that never left them. While this is true, they will often be left feeling even emptier and lower about themselves after giving into cravings.

Mood

A general low mood can cause emotional eating. While the problem of emotional eating is something that is occurring multiple times per week and we all have general low moods or bad days, if this makes you crave food and especially food of an unhealthy sort, this could become emotional eating. If every time we feel down or are having a bad day, we want to eat food to make ourselves feel better; this is emotional eating. Some people will have a bad day and want a drink at the end of the day, and if this happens every once in a while, it is not necessarily a problem with emotional eating. The more often it happens, the more often it is emotional eating. Further, we do not have to give in to the cravings for it to be considered emotional eating. Experiencing the cravings often and in tandem with negative feelings in the first place is what constitutes emotional eating.

Depression

Suffering from depression also can lead to emotional eating. Depression is a constant low mood for a period of months on end, and this low mood can cause a person to turn to food for comfort and a lift in spirit. This can then become emotional eating in addition to and because of depression.

Anxiety

Having anxiety can lead to emotional eating, as well. There are several types of anxiety, and whether it is general anxiety (constant levels of anxiety), situational anxiety (triggered by a situation or scenario), it can lead to emotional eating.

You have likely heard of the term *comfort food* to describe certain foods and dishes. The reason for this is because they are usually foods rich in carbohydrates, fats, and heavy in nature. These foods bring people a sense of comfort. These foods are often turned to when people suffering from anxiety are emotionally eating because these foods help to temporarily ease their anxiety and make them feel calmer and more at ease. This only lasts for a short period of time; however, before their anxiety usually gears up again.

Stress

Stress eating is probably the most common form of emotional eating. While this does not become an issue for everyone experiencing stress, and many people will do so every once in a while, it is a problem for those who consistently turn to food to ease their stress. Some people are always under stress, and they will constantly be looking for ways to ease their stress. Food is one of these ways that people use to make themselves feel better and to take their minds off of their stress. As with all of the other examples we have seen above, this is not a lasting resolution, and it becomes a cycle. Similar to the cycle diagram we saw above, the same can be used for stress except instead of a negative emotion and eating making you feel more down, stress eating can make you feel more stress as you feel like you have done something you shouldn't have which causes you stress, and the cycle ensues.

Recognizing your triggers is important because this will allow you to notice when you may be feeling emotional hunger and when you are feeling actual hunger. If you become hungry, you can look back on your day or on the last hour and determine if any of your triggers were present. If they were, then you will be able to determine that you are likely experiencing emotional hunger, and you can take the appropriate steps instead of giving in to the cravings blindly.

There are many different emotional causes for the cravings we experience. There may be others than those listed above, and these are all valid. A person's emotional eating experience is unique and personal and could be caused by any number of things. You may also experience a combination of emotional deficiencies listed above, or one of those listed above in addition to others. Many of these can overlap, such as anxiety and depression, which are often seen together in a single person. The level of these emotional deficiencies that you experience could indicate the level of emotional eating that you struggle with. Whatever your experience and your struggles though, there is hope of recovery, and this is what the rest of this book will focus on.

Chapter 3: How to Stop Binge Eating, Bulimia, and Emotional Eating

In this chapter, we are going to look at how you can begin to tackle your mind in order to make positive changes for your body and break free from your eating disorder once and for all.

Addressing the Core Wounds

The key to solving these food-related issues is to address your core wounds. Understanding how your mind works will help you to better take care of it. You will be able to recognize your feelings and how they could have come about, and then treat them in a way that will help it to feel better. Bettering your relationship with food and your body will also improve your relationship with your mind. This will then allow you to begin to feed it what it needs, which will, in turn, lead to better cognitive functioning, control over impulses, and decision-making. This will help overall in your relationship with your food, your body, and your mind.

What Are Core Wounds?

As we discussed in the previous chapter, there are several types of emotional deficiencies that can be indicated by disordered eating. Once you have determined which of these emotional deficiencies (or which combination of them) are present in your life, you can begin to look at them in a little more detail. By doing so, you will come upon your core wounds. A core wound is something that you believe to be true about yourself or your life, and it is something that likely came about as a result of a coping mechanism you developed to deal with childhood. For example, this could be something like; the feeling of not being enough, the belief that you are unlovable, or the belief that you are stupid.

How to Address Them

By understanding and addressing your core wounds, you will be able to change your behaviors because of the intricate relationship that exists between your thoughts, your emotions, and your behaviors. By addressing your thoughts and emotions, you will change your behaviors and thus, free yourself from disordered eating. You may be wondering how you can begin to address your core wounds, as it can be difficult to know where to begin.

The first step is learning how to control and change your thoughts, which in turn, leads to changes in your behavior. By taking control of your thoughts and your beliefs, they don't have the opportunity to manifest into unhealthy behaviors such as overeating, turning to food for comfort, or any other unhealthy coping mechanisms that you have developed over the course of your life.

Becoming aware of your own thoughts is the most crucial step in this entire guide, as everything else will fail without it. Paying attention to your thoughts will help you identify what thoughts are going through your mind during an intense emotional moment. By looking deep within, in order to get in touch with your deepest feelings, you will be more likely to succeed in your weight loss and your overall lifestyle improvement.

One great example of how to put this into practice is through the use of journaling. Journaling can help in a process such as this because it can help you to organize your thoughts and feelings and will help you to see visually what is working and what isn't working for you. While we can give tips and examples, every person is different, so to find exactly what works for you, you will have to try some different things and see which techniques help you personally the most and in the best way. Journaling can be about anything like how you feel since beginning a new program, how you feel physically since changing your diet, how you feel emotionally now that you are not reaching for food in order to comfort your emotions and anything along the lines of this.

Positive Self-Talk

Once you have addressed your emotions and your core wounds, you can begin to intervene and change them so that they result in healthier behaviors. You will do this using positive self-talk. Adopting helpful thought processes fosters better emotions overall, which leads to more productive behaviors.

When people have developed unhelpful thinking processes, it is hard to make decisions to benefit their future selves because their thoughts create negative emotions that drive away motivation. This is where something called *positive self-talk* can come in. Positive self-talk can be instrumental in helping you to recover from disordered eating.

What Is Positive Self-Talk?

Many people's minds are controlled by their inner critic. The inner critic shares words with you, such as "You should just give up" Or "What makes you think you'll succeed?" which is rooted in the opposite of positive self-talk- Negative self-talk!

Instead of creating an open space that allows for mistakes, growth, and development, your inner critic causes you to question your worth, which makes it difficult for you to have the positive, growth mindset that is needed to complete tasks and go after things that may be difficult to achieve. In this case, helping your mind to begin using positive self-talk will help you to recover for the long-term.

How to Use Positive Self-Talk?

Below are several ways that you can begin to use positive self-talk. Over time, your mind will get used to thinking in this way, and you will find it much easier to do.

1. Remind yourself

Bad habits are built through many years, and no amount of willpower can undo a lifetime of bad habits, such as a strong inner critic that uses negative self-talk. By rewiring your brain to minimize the amount of negativity you feel in the first place, you will eventually get used to filling your mind with positive thoughts instead of negative ones.

2. Stop the automatic process of negativity

Often times, if the person had just paid attention to their thought process, they would be able to catch themselves before their mind automatically spiraled to a place of complete de-motivation. By catching yourself before you get there, you can prevent yourself from falling into your negative thought patterns that are limiting you and holding you back.

3. Find positive influences

Surrounding yourself with people that can encourage you and foster positivity will also change your inner-critic's opinion. Often times, hearing positive compliments from other people hold a heavier weight in the eyes of your inner-critic compared to you telling your inner-critic the same thing. Try spending time with people who are supportive of your goals and the changes that you are looking to make in your life. It will make your journey a little bit easier.

4. Limit Negative Influences

By limiting the negative influences in your life, you are making a statement to yourself that you place importance on preserving your mental health. When you remove negative influences and limit your exposure to things or people that make you feel negative, you are prioritizing yourself, and this is a great way to practice self-care.

5. Practice a gratitude exercise

This is a great exercise to remind yourself of everything that you love and appreciate about yourself and your life. Take time to write down all of the things that you love about yourself and about your life. This will remind you of all of the positivity surrounding you and will serve to uplift you.

Chapter 4: Making Healthier Decisions Using Intuitive Eating

This chapter will provide you with a solid foundation of knowledge on which to build your new lifestyle. We will look at how intuitive eating can be the answer to all of your struggles and help you to find recovery.

Making Good Choices

As we discussed in the previous chapter, making good choices begins with self-exploration and a deep look into your core wounds. Once you have done this, you can begin to make decisions that are positive for your health and your life, and over time these will become more and more habitual. We are going to spend this chapter looking at some of the ways that you can begin to make good choices related to food and eating.

How to Begin Making Good Choices Using Intuitive Eating

One great way to make good choices when it comes to food is by using something called intuitive eating. Below, I will define intuitive eating for you and give you some insight into how this can change your life.

What Is Intuitive Eating?

Intuitive eating is a new perspective from which to view how you feed your body. This style of eating puts you in control, instead of following a list of pre-designed guidelines about when and what to eat. Intuitive eating instead encourages you to listen to your body and the signals it sends you about what, how much, and when to eat. This ensures that you are giving your body exactly what it needs when it needs it, instead of forcing it into a specific kind of diet.

Intuitive eating does not limit any specific foods and does not require you to stick to certain foods exclusively. Instead, it encourages you to learn as much as you can about what your body is telling you and follow its signals.

The two main components of the intuitive eating philosophy are the following; eat when you are hungry and stop eating when you are satiated. This may seem like a no-brainer, but in today's societies, we are very far from eating in an intuitive way, as odd as it may seem. With so many diet trends and numerous "rules" for how you should and should not eat, it can be difficult to put these ideas aside and let your body guide you exclusively.

Intuitive Eating and Hunger

Before we begin looking at the specifics of intuitive eating, we will look at the different types of hunger and how you can tell them apart. This will help you to distinguish when you are hungry and when you may be turning to food to soothe your emotional state.

Real hunger is when our body needs nutrients or energy and is letting us know that we should replenish our energy soon. This happens when it has been a few hours since our last meal when we wake up in the morning, or after a lot of strenuous activity like a long hike. Our body uses hunger to signal to us that it is in need of more energy and that if it doesn't get it soon, it will begin to use our stored energy as fuel. While there is nothing wrong with our body using its stored fuel, it can be used as a sign to us that we should eat shortly in order to replenish these stores. Perceived Hunger is when we think we are hungry, but our body doesn't actually require any more energy or for the stores to be replenished. This can happen for a number of reasons, including an emotional deficiency, a negative mental state, or the occurrence of a psychological trigger.

The philosophy behind intuitive eating is that if you wait until you are too hungry before eating, you will be much more likely to overeat or to binge eat. This is because, by this time, you be feeling ravenous instead of mildly hungry. If instead, you choose to adhere to your hunger and eat when your body tells you that it needs sustenance, you will be much more likely to eat just the right amount. As a result, your body will be satisfied rather than completely stuffed, and instead of feeling shameful and angry that you have eaten, you can feel happy that you have provided your body with what it needed. This requires you to listen to and respect what your body is telling you and then provide it with nutrients in order for it to keep working hard for you!

The Benefits of Intuitive Eating

One of the reasons that intuitive eating is such a successful and cherished form of eating is that it allows the body to lead the mind in the right direction when it comes to seeking out its needs. Below, we will look at the benefits of letting your body guide your eating choices.

- Allows the body to get what it needs

Did you know that your cravings could actually be giving you much more information than you give them credit for?
A craving is an intense longing for something (in this case food), that comes about intensely and feels urgent. In our case, that longing is for s a very specific type of food. When we have cravings for certain foods, it can actually mean more than what it seems.

While you may think that a craving is an indication of hunger or of a desire for the taste of a certain food, it may actually indicate that your body is low on certain vitamins or minerals. As a result, your body seeks out a certain food that it thinks will provide it with this vitamin or mineral. This reaches your consciousness in the form of an intense craving. In this case, the body is trying to help itself by telling you what to eat. For this reason, understanding your cravings could help you give your body exactly what it is longing for.

For example, if you are craving juice or pop or other sugary drinks like this, consider that you might actually be dehydrated and, therefore, thirsty. Sometimes we see drinks in our fridge, and since we are thirsty, we really want them. Next time you are craving a sugary drink, try having a glass of water first, then wait a few minutes and see if you are still craving that Coca-Cola. You may not want it anymore once your thirst is quenched.

If you are craving meat, you may feel like you want some fried chicken or a hot dog. This can indicate a deficit of iron or protein. The best sources of protein are chicken breast cooked in the oven, and iron is best received from spinach, oysters, or lentils. If you think you may not like these foods, there are many different ways to prepare them, and you can likely find a way that you like.

- Prevents overeating

It can be hard to know how much to eat and when you have had enough to eat without letting yourself eat too much. Sometimes people will eat until the point that they begin to feel completely full. Many times, we keep eating until we become stuffed, even to the point of making ourselves feel physically ill. Intuitive eating will help you to avoid this, as this kind of eating encourages you to give your body what it needs in order to take great care of it. Stuffing your body until it is too full is not what your body is asking for, and once you become accustomed to listening to your body's needs, you will know when it is time to stop.

- Helps you break free from self-judgment

intuitive eating will help you to finally make peace with your body and yourself as a whole. It does this by showing you that your body has needs and that there is no shame in tending to these needs, as long as you do so in a healthy way.

You cannot fully embrace and practice intuitive eating if you have those nagging feelings of self-judgment each time you take a bite of food or decide that you are going to eat lunch when you are hungry. For this reason, in order to practice intuitive eating, you must understand that feeding your body is an act of compassion for yourself and that this does not need to come with self-judgment.

- It is inclusive, not exclusive

One of the great things about this style of eating is that it is not founded on restricting a person's intake of certain foods or allowing only a small variety of foods.

Diets like this are extremely hard to transition to and are hard to maintain for a long period of time. Intuitive eating is about including as many natural whole foods as you wish, while also ensuring that you are consuming enough of all of your nutrients. With this style of eating, you can eat whatever you wish, whenever you wish. This makes it much easier to stick with this type of diet and reduces the chances of falling off after a short period of time due to cravings or intense hunger. It does not restrict calories or reduce your intake greatly, which makes it easier to handle than a traditional diet for many people. It feels natural to eat in this way, which makes it effective.

Chapter 5: Intuitive Eating Part 2

In this chapter, we are going to continue our examination of intuitive eating by looking at some more specific details related to this diet, as well as how to make it a regular part of your life.

How to Make Intuitive Eating Part of Your Life

One of the best ways to make this type of eating a part of your life is to practice it with intention. This is especially important when you are just beginning. Each time you feel a pang of hunger or a compulsion to eat, take a minute to examine your inner world. By doing this, you will get your mind and body accustomed to working together. In addition, do the same after you eat. By doing these two things, you will be able to ensure that you are eating when hungry and stopping when satisfied.

When you finish eating a meal, rank your level of fullness on a scale of 1 to 10, 1 being extremely hungry and 10 being extremely stuffed. This will help you to determine if you are successfully stopping when you are satisfied and not overeating.

It is also important that you learn how to deal with your emotions and feelings in an effective way without using food. Using the techniques that you have learned in this book, you will be able to address your inner demons, which will make space for you to listen to your body and its needs.

As you know by now, listening to your body, your emotions and your mind is extremely important when it comes to practicing intuitive eating. As long as you remember this, you will be well on your way to becoming a lifelong intuitive eater.

What Kind of Foods Should You Choose?

Fish is a great way to get healthy fats into your diet. Certain fish are very low in carbohydrates but high in good fats, making them perfect for a healthy diet. They also contain minerals and vitamins that will be good for your health. Salmon is a great fish to eat, as it is versatile and delicious. Many fish also include essential fatty acids that we can only get through our diet. Other fish that are good for you include:

- Sardines
- Mackerel
- Herring
- Trout
- Albacore Tuna

Meat and Poultry make up a large part of most Americans' diets. Meats and poultry that are fresh and not processed do not include any carbohydrates and contain high levels of protein. Eating lean meats helps to maintain your strength and muscle mass and gives you energy for hours. Grass-fed meats, in particular, are rich in antioxidants.

Eggs are another amazing, protein-filled food. Eggs help your body to feel satiated for longer and also keeps your blood sugar levels consistent, which is great for overall health. The whole egg is good for you, as the yolk is where the nutrients are. The cholesterol found within egg yolks also has been demonstrated to lower your risk of getting diseases like heart diseases, despite what most people think. Therefore, do not be afraid of the egg yolk!

Legumes are a great source of protein as well as fiber, and there are many different types to choose from. These include the following:

- All sorts of beans including black beans, green beans, and kidney beans
- Peas
- Lentils of all colors
- Chickpeas
- Peas

Examples of fruits that you can eat include the following:

- Citrus fruits such as oranges, grapefruits, lemons, and limes
- Melons of a variety of sorts
- Apples
- Bananas
- Berries including strawberries, blueberries, blackberries, raspberries and so on
- Grapes

Vegetables are a great source of energy and nutrients, and they include a wide range of naturally occurring vivid colors which should all be included in your diet.

- Carrots
- Broccoli and cauliflower
- Asparagus
- Kale
- All sorts of peppers including hot peppers, bell peppers
- Tomatoes
- Root vegetables (that are a good source of healthy, complete carbohydrates) such as potatoes, sweet potatoes, all types of squash, and beets.

Seeds are another great source of nutrients, vitamins, and minerals, and they are very versatile. These include the following:

- Sesame seeds
- Pumpkin seeds
- Sunflower seeds
- Hemp, flax and chia seeds are all especially good for your health

Nuts are a great way to get protein if you are choosing not to eat meat or if you are vegan. They also are packed with nutrients. Some examples are below.

- Almonds
- Brazil Nuts
- Cashews
- Macadamia nuts
- Pistachios
- Pecans

There are some **healthy fats** that are essential components of any person's diet, as the beneficial compounds that they contain cannot be made by our bodies; thus, we rely solely on or diet to get them. These compounds are Omega-3 Fatty Acids, monounsaturated and polyunsaturated fats. Below are some healthy sources of these compounds:

- Avocados
- Healthy, plant-based oils including olive oil and canola oil
- Hemp, chia and flax seeds
- Walnuts

When it comes to carbohydrates, these should be consumed in the form of **whole grains**, as they are high in fiber, which will help to prevent overeating. Whole grains also include essential minerals- those that we can only get from our diet just like those essential compounds found in healthy fats. These essential minerals are selenium, magnesium, and copper. Sources of these whole grains include the following:

- Quinoa
- Rye, Barley, buckwheat
- Whole grain oats
- Brown rice
- Whole grain bread can be hard to find these days in the grocery store, as many brown breads disguise themselves as whole grain when, in fact, they are not. However, there are whole grain breads if you take the time to look at the ingredients list.

Nutrients You Need and How to Get Them

In this section, we are going to look at the most beneficial nutrients for your body and where/ how you can find them. This will help you to decide which foods to include in your diet so that you can ensure you are getting all of the nutrients that your body needs.

　　1.　Omega-3 Fatty Acids

Some vitamins and nutrients are called "essential nutrients." Omega-3 Fatty Acids are an example of this type of nutrient. They are called essential nutrients because they cannot be made by our bodies; thus, they must be eaten in our diets. These fatty acids are a very specific type of fatty acid, and this type, in particular, is the most essential and the most beneficial for our brains and bodies.

They have numerous effects on the brain, including reducing inflammation (which reduces the risk of Alzheimer's) and maintaining and improving mood and cognitive function, including specifically memory. Omega-3's have these greatly beneficial effects because of the way that they act in the brain, which is what makes them so essential to our diets. Omega-3 Fatty Acids increase the production of new nerve cells in the brain by acting specifically on the nerve stem cells within the brain, causing new and healthy nerve cells to be generated.

Omega-3 fatty acids can be found in fish like salmon, sardines, black cod, and herring. It can also be taken as a pill-form supplement for those who do not eat fish or cannot eat enough of it. It can also be taken in the form of a fish oil supplement like krill oil.

Omega-3 is by far the most important nutrient that you need to ensure you are ingesting because of the numerous benefits that come from it, both in the brain and in the rest of the body. While supplements are often a last step when it comes to trying to include something in your diet, for Omega-3's, the benefits are too great to potentially miss by trying to receive all of it from your diet.

Magnesium

Magnesium is beneficial for your diet, as it also helps you to maintain strong bones and teeth. Magnesium and Calcium are most effective when ingested together, as Magnesium helps in the absorption of calcium. It also helps to reduce migraines and is great for calmness and relieving anxiety. Magnesium can be found in leafy green vegetables like kale and spinach, as well as fruits like bananas and raspberries, legumes like beans and chickpeas, vegetables like peas, cabbage, green beans, asparagus, and brussels sprouts, and fish like tuna and salmon.

Calcium

Calcium is beneficial for the healthy circulation of blood, and for maintaining strong bones and teeth. Calcium can come from dairy products like milk, yogurt, and cheese. It can also be found in leafy greens like kale and broccoli and sardines.

Chapter 6: How to Make These New Choices a

Habit

Now that you have learned a wealth of information about intuitive eating, we are going to look at some strategies that you can use to make these new, healthy choices a habit. This will take time, but by employing these strategies, you will surely find success.

Healthy Thinking Patterns

In this section, we will look at a real-life example of dealing with challenges to demonstrate healthy thinking patters when it comes to intuitive eating.

Let's say you are trying to focus on healthy eating, and you find that you have had trouble doing so. Maybe you ate a cupcake, or maybe you had a soda at breakfast. From the perspective of traditional diet mentality, this would become a problem for the diet, and this would become a problem in your mind as well. You would likely be beating yourself up and feeling terrible about the choice you have made.

Let's look at this example in more detail. It is very important to avoid beating yourself up or self-judging for falling off the wagon. This may happen sometimes. What we need to do though, is to focus not on the fact that it has happened, but on how we are going to deal with and react to it. There are a variety of reactions that a person may have to this type of situation. We will examine the possible reactions and their pros and cons below:

- You may feel as though your progress is ruined and that you might as well begin again another time. This could lead you to go back to your old ways and keep you from trying again for quite some time. This could happen many times, over and over again, and each time you slip up, you decide that you might as well give up this time and try again, but each time it ends the same.

- You may fall off of your plan and tell yourself that this day is a write-off and that you will begin again the next day. The problem with this method is that continuing the rest of the day as you would have before you decided to make a change will make it so that the next day is like beginning all over again, and it will be very hard to begin again. You may be able to begin again the next day, and it could be fine, but you must be able to really motivate yourself if you are going to do this. Knowing that you have fallen off before makes it so that you may feel down on yourself and feel as though you can't do it, so beginning again the next day is very important.

- The third option, similar to the previous case, you may fall off, but instead of deciding that the day is a write-off, you tell yourself that the entire week is a write-off, and you then decide that you will pick it up again the next week. This will be even harder than starting again the next day as multiple days of eating whatever you like will make it very hard to go back to making the healthy choices again afterward.

- After eating something that you wish you hadn't (and that wasn't a healthy choice), you decide not to eat anything for the rest of the day so that you don't eat too many calories or too much sugar, and decide that the next day you will start over again. This is very difficult on the body as you are going to be quite hungry by the time the evening rolls around. Instead of forgiving yourself, you are punishing yourself, and it will make it very hard not to reach for chips late at night when you are starving and feeling down.

- The fifth and final option is what you should do in this situation.

This option is the best for success and will make it the most likely that you will succeed long-term. If you fall off at lunch, let's say, because you are tired and, in a rush, and you just grab something from a fast-food restaurant instead of going home for lunch or buying something at the grocery store to eat, this is how we will deal with it. Firstly, you will likely feel like you have failed and may feel quite down about having made an unhealthy choice. Now instead of starving for the rest of the day or eating only lettuce for dinner, you will put this slip up at lunch behind you, and you will continue your day as if it never happened. You will eat a healthy dinner as you planned, and you will continue on with the plan. You will not wait until tomorrow to begin again; you will continue as you would if you had made that healthy choice at lunch. The key to staying on track is being able to bounce back. The people who can bounce back mentally are the ones who will be most likely to succeed. You will need to maintain a positive mental state and look forward to the rest of the day and the rest of the week in just the same way as you did before you had a slip-up. One bad meal out of the entire week is not going to ruin all of your progress and recovering from emotional eating is largely a mental game. It is more mental than anything else, so we must not underestimate the role that our mindset plays in our success or failure.

By using this type of thinking, you will set yourself up for success and will not fall off of your plan completely after one slip up.

Healthy Lifestyle Changes

One important way to ensure that these healthy choices stick for good is by changing some aspects of your lifestyle. By doing this, you will reduce the chances of slipping up by eliminating them altogether. For example, you can change the way you approach the grocery store.

When you are entering the grocery store, it is important that you change a few things about the way you shop, in order to set yourself up for success. This is especially important when you are just beginning your intuitive eating practice, as it will be challenging for you to enter the grocery store and avoid cravings and temptations.

The first thing to keep in mind when grocery shopping for a new diet is to enter with a list. By doing this, you are giving yourself a guide to follow, which will prevent you from picking up things that you are craving or things that you feel like eating in that moment.

One of the biggest things to keep in mind when beginning a new eating practice like intuitive eating is to avoid shopping when you are hungry. This will make you reach for anything and everything that you see. By entering the grocery store when you are satiated or when you have just eaten, you will be able to stick to your list and avoid falling prey to temptations.

If you treat your grocery shopping experience like a treasure hunt, you will be able to cross things off of the list one at a time without venturing to the parts of the grocery store that will prove to be a challenge for you to resist. If you are making healthy eating choices, you will likely be spending most of your time at the perimeter of the grocery store. This is where the whole, plant-based foods are located. By doing this, and entering with a list, you will be able to avoid the middle aisles where the processed, high-sugar temptation foods are all kept.

Having a plan is key when it comes to succeeding in learning new habits and employing a new lifestyle. This plan can be as detailed as you wish, or it can simply come in the form of a general overview. I recommend you start with a more detailed plan in the beginning as you ease into things.

As everyone is different, you may be the type of person who likes lots of lists and plans, or you may be the type of person who doesn't, but for everyone, beginning with a plan and following it closely for the first little while is best. For example, this plan can include things like what you will focus on each week, what you will reduce your intake of, and what you will try to achieve in terms of the mental work involved.

Once you have come up with a general plan for your new lifestyle and how you want it to look, you can then begin laying out more specific plans.

Planning your individual meals will make it much easier for you when you get home from work or when you wake up tired in the morning and need to pack something for your lunch.

You can plan your meals out a week in advance, two weeks or even a month if you wish. You can post this up on your fridge, and each day you will know exactly what you are eating, with no thinking required. This way, there won't be a chance for you to consider ordering a pizza or heating up some chicken fingers because you will already know exactly what you are going to make. By approaching your new style of eating in this way, you can make this transition easier on yourself and ensure success every step of the way.

30-Day Meal Plan

The following 30-day meal plan includes a variety of meals that you can make in order to keep your first thirty days interesting and tasty!

Day 1

- Breakfast:

Coffee

Feta, mushroom and spinach, omelet.

- Lunch:

Oven-baked tempeh with broccoli and cauliflower rice.

- Dinner:

Chicken Caesar salad- tofu and romaine lettuce, parmesan

Day 2

- Breakfast:

Unsweetened yogurt with a mix of some berries such as strawberries, raspberries, and some seeds like flax seeds and chia seeds, and nuts like sliced almonds and walnuts.

- Lunch:

A healthy lunch-time salad with avocado, cheese, grape tomatoes, and a variety of nuts and seeds like spicy pumpkin seeds. Add a salad dressing on top such as blue cheese or ranch dressing, or a homemade one using olive oil and garlic.

- Dinner:

Chicken breast with onions and a homemade tomato sauce. Served alongside some grilled zucchini or eggplant.

Day 3

- Breakfast:

A no sugar added full fat Greek yogurt bowl with seeds, nuts and berries.

1 Cup of coffee

- Lunch:

Make your own lunch box, including firm tofu or meat of some sort, raw tomatoes, any type of cheese cubes that you wish, pickles, a hard-boiled egg, vegetables such as celery, carrots, radishes or zucchini, nuts for protein and fat such as walnuts, or almonds, homemade guacamole (avocado, onion, garlic, jalapeno).

- Dinner:

Grilled portobello, grilled eggplant and grilled zucchini as well as cherry tomatoes sautéed in extra virgin olive oil with garlic. Served with rice and protein such as pork or chicken.

Day 4

- Breakfast:

Coffee

Homemade mushroom & Spinach Frittata, including any vegetables that you wish such as bell peppers and onion.

- Lunch:

Cream cheese with cucumber slices for dipping.

Hard-boiled egg

Meatballs with sweet and sour sauce

- Dinner

Bacon, Avocado, Lettuce, Tomato panini.

Day 5

- Breakfast:

Egg Salad with lettuce, cucumber and whole grain bread.

- Lunch:

Homemade guacamole (avocado, onion, garlic, jalapeno, lime juice) with raw zucchini slices for dipping.

Hard-boiled egg

Tuna

- Dinner:

Cauliflower gratin (cheese, cauliflower, onion, garlic and so on)

As well as chopped lettuce drizzled with Caesar Dressing

Day 6

- Breakfast:

Coffee with heavy cream or coconut oil.

Celery sticks, dipped in peanut or Almond Butter

- Lunch:

Leftover cauliflower gratin

As well as chopped lettuce drizzled with Caesar Dressing

- Dinner:

Cooked or raw broccoli with grated cheese on top

Steak seared in olive oil

Day 7

- Breakfast:

Pancakes with fresh fruits

Black Coffee

- Lunch:

Cold pasta salad with fresh vegetables

Feta and Tomato Meatballs

Raw fresh spinach

- Dinner:

Spicy Spaghetti Squash Casserole

Fresh spinach, raw or cooked with 1 Tbsp ranch dressing drizzled on top.

Day 8

- Breakfast

Smoothie

- Lunch

Tempeh meatballs with guacamole and raw vegetable salad

- Dinner

Rice noodle stir fry with your choice of vegetables and tofu

Day 9

- Breakfast

Omelet cooked in coconut oil with cheese, onions, bell pepper and tomatoes

- Lunch

Tofu scramble with vegetables such as spinach and mushrooms and cheese

- Dinner

Curry with chicken, rice and coconut milk sauce with hot chili paste

Day 10

- Breakfast

Full fat yogurt unsweetened with berries, chia seeds, flax seeds

- Lunch

Cobb salad with boiled egg, vegetables of your choice, tofu, tempeh or chicken and Caesar dressing

- Dinner

Homemade pizza with your choice of toppings

Day 11

- Breakfast

Smoothie with chia seeds and flax seeds, berries and plant-based protein powder, as well as plant-based milk

- Lunch

Salad with tofu or boiled egg, olive oil dressing, spinach and diced vegetables

- Dinner

Vegetarian frittata using coconut oil, spinach, mushroom, cheese, bell peppers and tomato

Day 12

- Breakfast

Greek yogurt no sugar added with nuts and seeds

- Lunch

Homemade tacos with your choice of toppings, including ground turkey

- Dinner

Macaroni and cheese with crumbled roasted bread crumbs on top

Day 13

- Breakfast

Whole grain oats with no sugar added, nuts, flax and chia seeds as well as heavy cream and a plant-based nut butter.

- Lunch

Lettuce wraps with curried tofu and grilled eggplant and zucchini

- Dinner

Homemade burritos filled with crumbled, seasoned meat of your choice, sour cream, guacamole and diced tomatoes

Day 14

- Breakfast

Greek yogurt no sugar added with nuts and seeds

- Lunch

Avocado egg bowls with bacon

- Dinner

Fried rice with your choice of vegetables, scrambled egg and tofu

Day 15

- Breakfast

Coffee with heavy cream and no sugar added

- Lunch

Carrots with guacamole, cottage cheese with nuts and seeds and homemade baked zucchini chips with olive oil drizzle

- Dinner

Egg Salad with Lettuce Wraps

Day 16

- Breakfast

Pancakes with no sugar added maple syrup

- Lunch

Vegetarian egg quiche with spinach and mushroom

- Dinner

Broccoli salad with onion, a cheese of your choice, creamy ranch dressing, almonds and walnuts sliced, as well as some avocado and tofu cubes

Day 17

- Breakfast

Potato hash browns fried in olive oil, sunny side up egg and tempeh "bacon" with a side of grilled tomatoes

- Lunch

Avocadoes stuffed with cauliflower "taco meat", homemade salsa with tomatoes and herbs, sour cream, and grated cheese

- Dinner

Cooked or raw broccoli

Small amount of butter that can be added to the broccoli for taste

Grated cheese on top that can also be added to the broccoli

With steak seared in olive oil

Day 18

- Breakfast

Shakshuka with eggs, tomatoes and parsley

- Lunch

Grilled zucchini roll ups with tomato and cheese

- Dinner

Coconut milk curry with rice, bell peppers and tofu

Day 19

- Breakfast

Breakfast smoothie with berries, no sugar added and full fat milk

- Lunch

Broccoli and cheese fritters with homemade hummus to dip and a side of carrots, celery and cucumber for dipping

- Dinner

Cobb salad including hard-boiled egg, ham cubes, your choice of vegetables and an olive oil or ranch dressing

Day 20

- Breakfast

Spinach and mushroom frittata

- Lunch

Sandwich with scrambled eggs, spinach and mushrooms cooked in olive oil and topped with lettuce, tomato or any other fillings or toppings you wish to include. Finally, add a homemade creamy avocado sauce with avocado, cilantro, pepper and salt and some sour cream.

- Dinner

Rice risotto with cheese, vegetable broth and mushrooms

Day 21

- Breakfast

Unsweetened yogurt with a mix of berries such as strawberries, raspberries, and some seeds like flax seeds and chia seeds, and nuts like sliced almonds and walnuts.

- Lunch

Caesar salad- dressing with no sugar added

Raw vegetables, mixed greens and tempeh

- Dinner

Cauliflower gratin- cheese, cauliflower and choice of vegetables

Day 22

- Breakfast

Hash browns fried in olive oil, sunny side up egg and bacon with a side of grilled tomatoes

- Lunch

Stuffed half zucchini with feta cheese, tomato sauce (no sugar added) and herbs for topping

- Dinner

Mashed potatoes using whole milk and cheese, with grilled eggplant and mushrooms

Day 23

- Breakfast

Nut butter smoothie with yogurt, nut butter, flax seeds, chia seeds

- Lunch

Pan fried steak seasoned with herbs and olive oil, paired with

A spinach salad with raw vegetables of choice and no sugar added Caesar dressing

- Dinner

Cauliflower pasta salad with celery, spinach, onions, and walnuts

Day 24

- Breakfast

Feta, mushroom and Spinach, omelet

Coffee

- Lunch

Coleslaw with a creamy cilantro dressing, carrots, cabbage, celery, tomato and herbs for topping

- Dinner

Crispy tofu cubes with zucchini noodles and a homemade peanut sauce

Day 25

- Breakfast

No bake protein bars

Coffee with no sugar added

- Lunch

Roasted tomatoes with goat cheese, spinach, cilantro and olive oil & balsamic drizzle

- Dinner

Eggplant and zucchini "French fries" with olive oil and crispy tofu cubes

Baked chicken breast

Day 26

- Breakfast

Pancakes with no sugar added maple syrup, full fat Greek yogurt and berries for topping

- Lunch

Low carb broccoli cheese soup with crispy cauliflower on the side

- Dinner

Curried rice with choice of vegetables, such as bell peppers and broccoli

Day 27

- Breakfast

Breakfast salad with scrambled egg, avocado, mixed greens, grilled tomatoes and cheese

- Lunch

Fried goat cheese with roasted red peppers, spinach and olive oil drizzle

- Dinner

Spicy Spaghetti Squash Casserole

Fresh spinach, raw or cooked with ranch dressing drizzled on top

Day 28

- Breakfast

Full fat yogurt unsweetened with berries, chia seeds, flax seeds

- Lunch

Vegetarian chili with tomato, sour cream, a variety of beans and tomatoes

- Dinner

Zucchini spiral pasta noodles with creamy yogurt avocado sauce

Day 29

- Breakfast

Cauliflower "bread" grilled cheese sandwich (similar to cauliflower crust pizza but made as a grilled cheese sandwich instead.

- Lunch

Green beans with mushrooms and tomatoes with a chicken breast on the side

- Dinner

Grape tomato marinara on pasta noodles with parmigiano Reggiano cheese and fresh cracked pepper.

Day 30

- Breakfast

Egg taco shells filled with choice of vegetables

- Lunch

Baked crispy tofu steaks with a sesame seed crust on a bed of zucchini strips and spinach

- Dinner

Baked Spaghetti squash filled with roasted tomatoes and eggplant, topped with melted, crispy cheese

Chapter 7: What to Do Next

As you take all of this information forth with you, it may seem overwhelming to begin applying this to your own life. Remember, life is a process, and you do not need to expect perfection from yourself right away. By taking the first step- reading this book, you are already on your way to changing your life. If you fall off and find that you are back to your old ways, try to find inspiration in the pages of this book once again. If you find that you are unable to find success on your own, there is no shame in seeking professional help. There are many people who are trained professionals in dealing with disordered eating and who can serve as a mentor or a guide for you as you navigate this challenge.

How To Seek Help If It Becomes Uncontrollable?

Understanding and accepting that you need help is the first step to recovery. By reading this book, you have taken this step. If you need further help, there is no shame in accepting this fact. There are many ways to seek help for disordered eating, depending on the level of help that you need. Below is a list of ways that you can seek help, ordered from least to most help.

- Online resources
- Support System
- Support Group
- Group counseling
- Anonymous online counseling or telephone counseling
- One on One counseling

- Talk therapy
- Rehab centers

Counseling or Therapy

Talking therapies are very effective treatments for disordered eating. The things that people learn in therapy gives them the insight and skills in order to feel better and tackle their eating disorder, as well as to prevent it from coming back in the future.

One example of talk therapy is Cognitive Behavioral Therapy or CBT. The way that cognitive behavioral therapy works is by putting an emphasis on the relationship between a person's thoughts, emotions, and behaviors. The theory behind this is that when a person changes any one of these components, change will be initiated in the others. The goal of CBT is to help a person decrease negative thoughts or the amount of worry they experience in order to increase their overall quality of life.

If you think that this is something you would benefit from, please reach out to your local resources to find out more.

PART II

In this chapter, we are going to study the details of the reset diet and what recipes you can make.

Chapter 1: How to Reset Your Body?

Created by a celebrity trainer, Harley Pasternak, the body reset diet is a famous fifteen-day eating pattern that aims to jump-start weight loss. According to Pasternak, if you experience rapid loss in weight early in a diet, you will feel more motivated to stick to that diet plan. This theory is even supported by a few scientific studies (Alice A Gibson, 2017).

The body reset diet claims to help in weight loss with light exercise and low-calorie diet plans for fifteen days. The diet is divided into 3 phases of five days each. Each phase had a particular pattern of diet and exercise routine. You need to consume food five times every day, starting from the first phase, which mostly consists of smoothies and progressing to more solid foods in the second and third phases.

The three phases of the body reset diet are:

- **Phase One** – During this stage, you are required to consume only two snacks every day and drink smoothies for breakfast, lunch, and dinner. In the case of exercise, you have to walk at least ten thousand steps per day.

- **Phase Two** – During this phase, you can eat two snacks each day, consume solid food only once, and have to replace any two meals of the day with smoothies. In case of exercise, apart from walking ten thousand steps every day, on three of the days, you also have to finish five minutes of resistance training with the help of four separate exercises.

- **Phase Three** – You can consume two snacks every day, but you have to eat two low-calorie meals and replace one of your meals with a smoothie. For exercise, you are required to walk ten thousand steps. Apart from that, you also have to finish five minutes of resistance training with the help of four separate exercises each day.

After you have finished the standard fifteen-day diet requirements, you have to keep following the meal plan you followed in the third phase. However, during this time, you are allowed to have two "free meals" twice a week in which you can consume anything you want. These "free meals" are meant as a reward so that you can avoid feeling deprived. According to Pasternak, depriving yourself of a particular food continuously can result in binge eating (Nawal Alajmi, 2016).

There is no official endpoint of the diet after the first fifteen days for losing and maintaining weight. Pasternak suggests that the habits and routines formed over fifteen days should be maintained for a lifetime.

Chapter 2: Science Behind Metabolism Reset

Several people take on a "cleanse" or "detox" diet every year to lose the extra holiday weight or simply start following healthy habits. However, some fat diet plans are often a bit overwhelming. For example, it requires a tremendous amount of self-discipline to drink only juices. Moreover, even after finishing a grueling detox diet plan, you might just go back to eating foods that are bad for you because of those days of deprivation. New studies issued in the *Medicine & Science in Sports & Exercise* shows that low-calorie diets may result in binge eating, which is not the right method for lasting weight loss.

Another research conducted by the researchers at Loughborough University showed that healthy, college-aged women who followed a calorie-restricted diet consumed an extra three hundred calories at dinner as compared to the control group who consumed three standard meals. They revealed that it was because they had lower levels of peptide YY (represses appetite) and higher levels of ghrelin (makes you hungry). They are most likely to go hog wild when you are feeling ravenous, and it's finally time to eat (Nawal Alajmi K. D.-O., 2016).

Another research published in *Cognitive Neuroscience* studied the brains of chronic dieters. They revealed that there was a weaker connection between the two regions of the brain in people who had a higher percentage of body fat. They showed that they might have an increased risk of getting obese because it's harder for them to set their temptations aside (Pin-Hao Andy Chen, 2016).

A few other studies, however, also revealed that you could increase your self-control through practice. Self-control, similar to any other kind of strength, also requires time to develop. However, you can consider focusing on a diet plan that can help you "reset" instead of putting all your efforts into developing your self-control to get healthy.

A reset is considered as a new start – one that can get your metabolism and your liver in good shape. The liver is the biggest solid organ of your body, and it's mainly responsible for removing toxins that can harm your health and well-being by polluting your system. Toxins keep accumulating in your body all the time, and even though it's the liver's job to handle this, it can sometimes get behind schedule, which can result in inflammation. It causes a lot of strain on your metabolism and results in weight gain, particularly around the abdomen. The best method to alleviate this inflammation is to follow a metabolism rest diet and give your digestive system a vacation (Olivia M. Farr, 2015).

Chapter 3: Recipes for Smoothies and Salads

If you want to lose weight and you have a particular period within which you want to achieve it, then here are some recipes that are going to be helpful.

Green Smoothie

Total Prep & Cooking Time: 2 minutes

Yields: 1 serving

Nutrition Facts: Calories: 144 | Carbs: 28.2g | Protein: 3.4g | Fat: 2.9g | Fiber: 4.8g

Ingredients:

- One cup each of
    - Almond milk
    - Raw spinach
- One-third of a cup of strawberries
- One orange, peeled

Method:

1. Add the peeled orange, strawberries, almond milk, and raw spinach in a blender and blend everything until you get a smooth paste. You can add extra water if required to achieve the desired thickness.

2. Pour out the smoothie into a glass and serve.

Strawberry Banana Smoothie

Total Prep & Cooking Time: 5 minutes

Yields: 2 servings

Nutrition Facts: Calories: 198| Carbs: 30.8g | Protein: 5.9g | Fat: 7.1g | Fiber: 4.8g

Ingredients:

- Half a cup each of
    - Milk
    - Greek yogurt
- One banana, frozen and quartered
- Two cups of fresh strawberries, halved

Method:

1. Add the milk, Greek yogurt, banana, and strawberries into a high-powered blender and blend until you get a smooth mixture.
2. Pour the smoothie equally into two separate glasses and serve.

Notes:

- *Don't add ice to the smoothie as it can make it watery very quickly. Using frozen bananas will keep your smoothie cold.*

- *As you're using bananas and strawberries, there is no need to add any artificial sweetener.*

Salmon Citrus Salad

Total Prep & Cooking Time: 20 minutes

Yields: 6 servings

Nutrition Facts: Calories: 336 | Carbs: 20g | Protein: 17g | Fat: 21g | Fiber: 5g

Ingredients:

- One pound of Citrus Salmon (slow-roasted)
- Half of an English cucumber, sliced
- One tomato (large), sliced into a quarter of an inch thick pieces
- One grapefruit, peeled and cut into segments
- Two oranges, peeled and cut into segments
- Three beets, roasted and quartered
- One avocado
- Boston lettuce leaves
- Two tablespoons of red wine vinegar
- Half of a red onion
- Flakey salt
- Aleppo pepper flakes

For the Citrus Shallot Vinaigrette,

- Five tablespoons of olive oil (extra-virgin)
- One clove of garlic, smashed
- Salt and pepper
- One and a half tablespoons of rice wine vinegar
- Two tablespoons of orange juice or fresh lemon juice
- One tablespoon of shallot, minced

Method:

For preparing the Citrus Shallot Vinaigrette:

1. Add the ingredients for the vinaigrette in a bowl and whisk them together.
2. Keep the mixture aside.

For assembling the salad,

1. Add the onions and vinegar in a small bowl and pickle them by letting them sit for about fifteen minutes.
2. In the meantime, place the lettuce leaves on the serving plate.
3. Dice the avocado in half and eliminate the pit. Then scoop the flesh and add them onto the plate. Sprinkle a dash of flakey salt and Aleppo pepper on top to season it.

4. Add the quartered beets onto the serving plate along with the grapefruit and orange segments.

5. Salt the cucumber and tomato slices lightly and add them onto the plate.

6. Then, scatter the pickled onions on top and cut the salmon into bits and add it on the plate.

7. Lastly, drizzle the Citrus Shallot Vinaigrette on top of the salad and finish off with a dash of flakey salt.

Chapter 4: Quick and Easy Breakfast and Main Course Recipes

Quinoa Salad

Total Prep & Cooking Time: 40 minutes

Yields: Eight servings

Nutrition Facts: Calories: 205 | Carbs: 25.9g | Protein: 6.1g | Fat: 9.4g | Fiber: 4.6g

Ingredients:

- One tablespoon of red wine vinegar
- One-fourth of a cup each of
    - Lemon juice (about two to three lemons)
    - Olive oil
- One cup each of
    - Quinoa (uncooked), rinsed with the help of a fine-mesh colander
    - Flat-leaf parsley (from a single large bunch), finely chopped
- Three-fourth of a cup of red onion (one small red onion), chopped
- One red bell pepper (medium-sized), chopped
- One cucumber (medium-sized), seeded and chopped

- One and a half cups of chickpeas (cooked), or One can of chickpeas (about fifteen ounces), rinsed and drained
- Two cloves of garlic, minced or pressed
- Two cups of water
- Black pepper, freshly ground
- Half a teaspoon of fine sea salt

Method:

1. Place a medium-sized saucepan over medium-high heat and add the rinsed quinoa into it along with the water. Allow the mixture to boil and then reduce the heat and simmer it. Cook for about fifteen minutes so that the quinoa has absorbed all the water. As time goes on, decrease the heat and maintain a gentle simmer. Take the saucepan away from the heat and cover it with a lid. Allow the cooked quinoa to rest for about five minutes to give it some time to increase in size.

2. Add the onions, bell pepper, cucumber, chickpeas, and parsley in a large serving bowl and mix them together. Keep the mixture aside.

3. Add the garlic, vinegar, lemon juice, olive oil, and salt in another small bowl and whisk the ingredients so that they are appropriately combined. Keep this mixture aside.

4. When the cooked quinoa has almost cooled down, transfer it to the serving bowl. Add the dressing on top and toss to combine everything together.

5. Add an extra pinch of sea salt and the black pepper to season according to your preference. Allow the salad to rest for five to ten minutes before serving it for the best results.

6. You can keep the salad in the refrigerator for up to four days. Make sure to cover it properly.

7. You can serve it at room temperature or chilled.

Notes: *Instead of cooking additional quinoa, you can use about three cups of leftover quinoa for making this salad. Moreover, you can also serve this salad with fresh greens and an additional drizzle of lemon juice and olive oil. You can also add a dollop of cashew sour cream or crumbled feta cheese as a topping.*

Herb and Goat Cheese Omelet

Total Prep & Cooking Time: 20 minutes

Yields: Two servings

Nutrition Facts: Calories: 233 | Carbs: 3.6g | Protein: 16g | Fat: 17.6g | Fiber: 1g

Ingredients:

- Half a cup each of
    - Red bell peppers (3 x quarter-inch), julienne-cut
    - Zucchini, thinly sliced
- Four large eggs
- Two teaspoons of olive oil, divided
- One-fourth of a cup of goat cheese (one ounce), crumbled
- Half a teaspoon of fresh tarragon, chopped
- One teaspoon each of
    - Fresh parsley, chopped
    - Fresh chives, chopped
- One-eighth of a teaspoon of salt
- One-fourth of a teaspoon of black pepper, freshly ground (divided)
- One tablespoon of water

Method:

1. Break the eggs into a bowl and add one tablespoon of water into it. Whisk them together and add in one-eighth of a teaspoon each of salt and ground black pepper.

2. In another small bowl, mix the goat cheese, tarragon, and parsley and keep it aside.

3. Place a nonstick skillet over medium heat and heat one teaspoon of olive oil in it. Add in the sliced zucchini, bell pepper, and the remaining one-eighth of a teaspoon of black pepper along with a dash of salt. Cook for about four minutes so that the bell pepper and zucchini get soft. Transfer the zucchini-bell pepper mixture onto a plate and cover it with a lid to keep it warm.

4. Add about half a teaspoon of oil into a skillet and add in half of the whisked egg into it. Do not stir the eggs and let the egg set slightly. Loosen the set edges of the omelet carefully with the help of a spatula. Tilt the skillet to move the uncooked part of the egg to the side. Keep following this method for about five seconds so that there is no more runny egg in the skillet. Add half of the crumbled goat cheese mixture evenly over the omelet and let it cook for another minute so that it sets.

5. Transfer the omelet onto a plate and fold it into thirds.

6. Repeat the process with the rest of the egg mixture, half a teaspoon of olive oil, and the goat cheese mixture.

7. Add the chopped chives on top of the omelets and serve with the bell pepper and zucchini mixture.

Mediterranean Cod

Total Prep & Cooking Time: 15 minutes

Yields: 4 servings

Nutrition Facts: Calories: 320 | Carbs: 31g | Protein: 35g | Fat: 8g | Fiber: 8g

Ingredients:

- One pound of spinach
- Four fillets of cod (almost one and a half pounds)
- Two zucchinis (medium-sized), chopped
- One cup of marinara sauce
- One-fourth of a teaspoon of red pepper, crushed
- Two cloves of garlic, chopped
- One tablespoon of olive oil
- Salt and pepper, according to taste
- Whole wheat roll, for serving

Method:

1. Place a ten-inch skillet on medium heat and add the marinara sauce and zucchini into it. Combine them together and let it simmer on medium heat.

2. Add the fillets of cod into the simmering sauce. Add one-fourth of a teaspoon each of salt and pepper too. Cover the skillet with a lid and let it cook for about seven minutes so that the cod gets just opaque throughout.

3. In the meantime, place a five-quart saucepot on medium heat and heat the olive oil in it. Add in the crushed red pepper and minced garlic. Stir and cook for about a minute.

4. Then, add in the spinach along with one-eighth of a teaspoon of salt. Cover the saucepot with a lid and let it cook for about five minutes, occasionally stirring so that the spinach gets wilted.

5. Add the spinach on the plates and top with the sauce and cod mixture and serve with the whole wheat roll.

Grilled Chicken and Veggies

Total Prep & Cooking Time: 35 minutes

Yields: 4 servings

Nutrition Facts: Calories: 305 | Carbs: 11g | Protein: 26g | Fat: 17g | Fiber: 3g

Ingredients:

For the marinade,

- Four cloves of garlic, crushed
- One-fourth of a cup each of
    - Fresh lemon juice
    - Olive oil
- One teaspoon each of
    - Salt
    - Smoked paprika
    - Dried oregano
- Black pepper, according to taste
- Half a teaspoon of red chili flakes

For the grilling,

- Two to three zucchinis or courgette (large), cut into thin slices

- Twelve to sixteen spears of asparagus, woody sides trimmed
- Broccoli
- Two bell peppers, seeds eliminated and cut into thin slices
- Four pieces of chicken breasts (large), skinless and de-boned

Method:

1. Preheat your griddle or grill pan.

2. Sprinkle some salt on top of the chicken breasts to season them. Keep them aside to rest while you prepare the marinade.

3. For the marinade, mix all the ingredients properly.

4. Add about half of the marinade over the vegetables and the other half over the seasoned chicken breasts. Allow the marinade to rest for a couple of minutes.

5. Place the chicken pieces on the preheated grill. Grill for about five to seven minutes on each side until they are cooked according to your preference. The time on the grill depends on the thickness of the chicken breasts.

6. Remove them from the grill and cover them using a foil. Set it aside to rest and prepare to grill the vegetables in the meantime.

7. Grill the vegetables for a few minutes until they begin to char and are crispy yet tender.

8. Remove them from the grill and transfer them onto a serving plate. Serve the veggies along with the grilled chicken and add the lemon wedges on the side for squeezing.

Notes: *You can add as much or as little vegetables as you like. The vegetable amounts are given only as a guide. Moreover, feel free to replace some of them with the vegetables you like to eat.*

Stuffed Peppers

Total Prep & Cooking Time: 50 minutes

Yields: 4 servings

Nutrition Facts: Calories: 438 | Carbs: 32g | Protein: 32g | Fat: 20g | Fiber: 5g

Ingredients:

For the stuffed peppers,

- One pound of ground chicken or turkey
- Four bell peppers (large) of any color
- One and a quarter of a cups of cheese, shredded
- One and a half cups of brown rice, cooked (you can use cauliflower rice or quinoa)
- One can (about fourteen ounces) of fire-roasted diced tomatoes along with its juices
- Two teaspoons of olive oil (extra-virgin)
- One teaspoon each of
    - Garlic powder
    - Ground cumin
- One tablespoon of ground chili powder
- One-fourth of a teaspoon of black pepper
- Half a teaspoon of kosher salt

For serving,

- Sour cream or Greek yogurt
- Salsa
- Freshly chopped cilantro
- Avocado, sliced
- Freshly squeezed lemon juice

Method:

1. Preheat your oven to 375 degrees Fahrenheit.

2. Take a nine by thirteen-inch baking dish and coat it lightly with a nonstick cooking spray.

3. Take the bell peppers and slice them from top to bottom into halves. Remove the membranes and the seeds. Keep the bell peppers in the baking dish with the cut-side facing upwards.

4. Place a large, nonstick skillet on medium-high heat and heat the olive oil in it. Add in the chicken, pepper, salt, garlic powder, ground cumin, and chili powder and cook for about four minutes so that the chicken is cooked through and gets brown. Break apart the chicken while it's cooking. Drain off any excess liquid and then add in the can of diced tomatoes along with the juices. Allow it to simmer for a minute.

5. Take the pan away from the heat. Add in the cooked rice along with three-fourth of a cup of the shredded cheese and stir everything together.

6. Add this filling inside the peppers and add the remaining shredded cheese as a topping.

7. Add a little amount of water into the pan containing the peppers so that it barely covers the bottom of the pan.

8. Keep it uncovered and bake it in the oven for twenty-five to thirty-five minutes so that the cheese gets melted and the peppers get soft.

9. Add any of your favorite fixings as a topping and serve hot.

Notes:

- *For preparing the stuffed peppers ahead of time, make sure to allow the rice and chicken mixture to cool down completely before filling the peppers. You can prepare the stuffed peppers before time, and then you have to cover it with a lid and keep it in the refrigerator for a maximum of twenty-four hours before baking the peppers.*

- *If you're planning to reheat the stuffed peppers, gently reheat them in your oven or microwave. If you're using a microwave for this purpose, make sure to cut the peppers into pieces to warm them evenly.*

- *You can store any leftovers in the freezer for up to three months. Alternatively, you can keep them in the refrigerator for up to four days. Allow it to thaw in the fridge overnight.*

Brussels Sprouts With Honey Mustard Chicken

Total Prep & Cooking Time: Fifty minutes

Yields: Four servings

Nutrition Facts: Calories: 360 | Carbs: 14.5g | Protein: 30.8g | Fat: 20g | Fiber: 3.7g

Ingredients:

- One and a half pounds of Brussels sprouts, divided into two halves
- Two pounds of chicken thighs, skin-on and bone-in (about four medium-sized thighs)
- Three cloves of garlic, minced
- One-fourth of a large onion, cut into slices
- One tablespoon each of
    - Honey
    - Whole-grain mustard
    - Dijon mustard
- Two tablespoons of freshly squeezed lemon juice (one lemon)
- One-fourth of a cup plus two tablespoons of olive oil (extra-virgin)
- Freshly ground black pepper
- Kosher salt
- Non-stick cooking spray

Method:

1. Preheat your oven to 425 degrees Fahrenheit.

2. Take a large baking sheet and grease it with nonstick cooking spray. Keep it aside.

3. Add the minced garlic, honey, whole-grain mustard, Dijon mustard, one tablespoon of the lemon juice, one-fourth cup of the olive oil in a medium-sized bowl and mix them together. Add the Kosher salt and black pepper to season according to your preference.

4. Dip the chicken thighs into the sauce with the help of tongs and coat both sides. Transfer the things on the baking sheet. You can get rid of any extra sauce.

5. Mix the red onion and Brussels sprouts in a medium-sized bowl and drizzle one tablespoon of lemon juice along with the remaining two tablespoons of olive oil onto it. Toss everything together until the vegetables are adequately coated.

6. Place the red onion-Brussels sprouts mixture on the baking sheet around the chicken pieces. Ensure that the chicken and vegetables are not overlapping.

7. Sprinkle a little amount of salt and pepper on the top and keep it in the oven to roast for about thirty to thirty-five minutes so that the Brussels sprouts get crispy and the chicken has an internal

temperature of 165 degrees Fahrenheit and has turned golden brown.

8. Serve hot.

Quinoa Stuffed Chicken

Total Prep & Cooking Time: 50 minutes

Yields: Four servings

Nutrition Facts: Calories: 355 | Carbs: 28g | Protein: 30g | Fat: 13g | Fiber: 4g

Ingredients:

- One and a half cups of chicken broth
- Three-fourths of a cup of quinoa (any color of your choice)
- Four chicken breasts (boneless and skinless)
- One lime, zested and one tablespoon of lime juice
- One-fourth of a cup of cilantro, chipped
- One-third of a cup of unsweetened coconut, shaved or coconut chips
- One Serrano pepper, seeded and diced
- Two cloves of garlic, minced
- Half a cup of red onion, diced
- Three-fourth of a cup of bell pepper, diced
- One tablespoon of coconut oil
- One teaspoon each of
    - Salt
    - Chili powder
    - Ground cumin

Method:

1. Preheat your oven to 375 degrees Fahrenheit.

2. Take a rimmed baking sheet and line it with parchment paper.

3. Place a medium-sized saucepan over medium-high heat and add the coconut oil in it. After it has melted, add in the Serrano peppers, garlic, red onion, and bell pepper and sauté for about one to two minutes so that they soften just a bit. Make sure that the vegetables are still bright in color. Then transfer the cooked vegetables into a bowl.

4. Add the quinoa in the empty sauce pot and increase the heat to high. Pour the chicken broth in it along with half a teaspoon of salt. Close the lid of the pot and bring it to a boil, allowing the quinoa to cook for about fifteen minutes so that the surface of the quinoa develops vent holes, and the broth has absorbed completely. Take the pot away from the heat and allow it to steam for an additional five minutes.

5. In the meantime, cut a slit along the long side in each chicken breast. It will be easier with the help of a boning knife. You are making a deep pocket in each breast, having a half-inch border around the remaining three attached sides. Keep the knife parallel to the cutting board and cut through the middle of the breast and

leaving the opposite side attached. Try to cut it evenly as it's challenging to cook thick uncut portions properly in the oven. After that, add salt, cumin, and chili powder on all sides of the chicken.

6. When the quinoa has turned fluffy, add in the lime juice, lime zest, shaved coconut, and sautéed vegetables and stir them in. Taste the mixture and adjust the salt as per your preference.

7. Add the confetti quinoa mixture inside the cavity of the chicken breast. Place the stuffed breasts on the baking sheet with the quinoa facing upwards. They'll look like open envelopes.

8. Bake them in the oven for about twenty minutes.

9. Serve warm.

Kale and Sweet Potato Frittata

Total Prep & Cooking Time: 30 minutes

Yields: 4 servings

Nutrition Facts: Calories: 144 | Carbs: 10g | Protein: 7g | Fat: 9g | Fiber: 2g

Ingredients:

- Three ounces of goat cheese
- Two cloves of garlic
- Half of a red onion (small)
- Two cups each of
    - Sweet potatoes
    - Firmly packed kale, chopped
- Two tablespoons of olive oil
- One cup of half-and-half
- Six large eggs
- Half a teaspoon of pepper, freshly ground
- One teaspoon of Kosher salt

Method:

1. Preheat your oven to 350 degrees Fahrenheit.

2. Add the eggs, half-and-half, salt, and black pepper in a bowl and whisk everything together.

3. Place a ten-inch ovenproof nonstick skillet over medium heat and add one tablespoon of oil in it. Sauté the sweet potatoes in the skillet for about eight to ten minutes so that they turn soft and golden brown. Transfer them onto a plate and keep warm.

4. Next, add in the remaining one tablespoon of oil and sauté the kale along with the red onions and garlic in it for about three to four minutes so that the kale gets soft and wilted. Then, add in the whisked egg mixture evenly over the vegetables and cook for an additional three minutes.

5. Add some goat cheese on the top and bake it in the oven for ten to fourteen minutes so that it sets.

Walnut, Ginger, and Pineapple Oatmeal

Total Prep & Cooking Time: 30 minutes

Yields: 4 servings

Nutrition Facts: Calories: 323 | Carbs: 61g | Protein: 6g | Fat: 8g | Fiber: 5g

Ingredients:

- Two large eggs
- Two cups each of
    - Fresh pineapple, coarsely chopped
    - Old-fashioned rolled oats
    - Whole milk
- One cup of walnuts, chopped
- Half a cup of maple syrup
- One piece of ginger
- Two teaspoons of vanilla extract
- Half a teaspoon of salt

Method:

1. Preheat your oven to 400 degrees Fahrenheit.

2. Add the ginger, walnuts, pineapple, oats, and salt in a large bowl and mix them together. Add the mixture evenly among four ten-ounce ramekins and keep them aside.

3. Whisk the eggs along with the milk, maple syrup, and vanilla extract in a medium-sized bowl. Pour one-quarter of this mixture into each ramekin containing the oat-pineapple mixture.

4. Keep the ramekins on the baking sheet and bake them in the oven for about twenty-five minutes until the oats turn light golden brown on the top and have set properly.

5. Serve with some additional maple syrup on the side.

Caprese Salad

Total Prep & Cooking Time: 15 minutes

Yields: 4 servings

Nutrition Facts: Calories: 216 | Carbs: 4g | Protein: 13g | Fat: 16g | Fiber: 1g

Ingredients:

For the salad,

- Nine basil leaves (medium-sized)
- Eight ounces of fresh whole-milk mozzarella cheese
- Two tomatoes (medium-sized)
- One-fourth of a teaspoon of black pepper, freshly ground
- Half a teaspoon of Kosher salt, or one-fourth of a teaspoon of sea salt

For the dressing,

- One teaspoon of Dijon mustard
- One tablespoon each of
    - Balsamic vinegar

- Olive oil

Method:

1. Add the olive oil, balsamic vinegar, and Dijon mustard into a small bowl and whisk them together with the help of a small hand whisk so that you get a smooth salad dressing. Keep it aside.

2. Cut the tomatoes into thin slices and try to get ten slices in total.

3. Cut the mozzarella into nine thin slices with the help of a sharp knife.

4. Place the slices of tomatoes and mozzarella on a serving plate, alternating and overlapping one another. Then, add the basil leaves on the top.

5. Season the salad with black pepper and salt and drizzle the prepared dressing on top.

6. Serve immediately.

One-Pot Chicken Soup

Total Prep & Cooking Time: 30 minutes

Yields: 6 servings

Nutrition Facts: Calories: 201 | Carbs: 20g | Protein: 16g | Fat: 7g | Fiber: 16g

Ingredients:

- Three cups of loosely packed chopped kale (or other greens of your choice)
- Two cups of chicken, shredded
- One can of white beans (about fifteen ounces), slightly drained
- Eight cups of broth (vegetable broth or chicken broth)
- Four cloves of garlic, minced
- One cup of yellow or white onion, diced
- One tablespoon of avocado oil (skip if you are using bacon)
- One strip of uncured bacon, chopped (optional)
- Black pepper + sea salt, according to taste

Method:

1. Place a Dutch oven or a large pot over medium heat. When it gets hot, add in the oil or bacon (optional), stirring occasionally, and allow it to get hot for about a minute.

2. Then, add in the diced onion and sauté for four to five minutes, occasionally stirring so that the onions get fragrant and translucent. Add in the minced garlic next and sauté for another two to three minutes. Be careful so as not to burn the ingredients.

3. Then, add the chicken, slightly drained white beans, and broth and bring the mixture to a simmer. Cook for about ten minutes to bring out all the flavors. Taste the mixture and add salt and pepper to season according to your preference. Add in the chopped kale in the last few minutes of cooking. Cover the pot and let it cook until the kale has wilted.

4. Serve hot.

Notes: *You can store any leftovers in the freezer for up to a month. Or, you can store them in the refrigerator for a maximum of three to four days. Simply reheat on the stovetop or in the microwave and eat it later.*

Chocolate Pomegranate Truffles

Total Prep & Cooking Time: 10 minutes

Yields: Twelve to Fourteen truffles

Nutrition Facts: Calories: 95 | Carbs: 26g | Protein: 1g | Fat: 2g | Fiber: 3g

Ingredients:

- One-third of a cup of pomegranate arils
- Half a teaspoon each of
    - Vanilla extract
    - Ground cinnamon
- Half a cup of ground flax seed
- Two tablespoons of cocoa powder (unsweetened)
- About one tablespoon of water
- One and a half cups of pitted Medjool dates
- One-eighth of a teaspoon of salt

Method:

1. Add the pitted dates in a food processor and blend until it begins to form a ball. Add some water and pulse again. Add in the vanilla,

cinnamon, flax seeds, cocoa powder, and salt and blend until everything is combined properly.

2. Turn off the food processor and unplug it. Add in the pomegranate arils and fold them in the mixture so that they are distributed evenly.

3. Make twelve to fourteen balls using the mixture. You can create an outer coating or topping if you want by rolling the balls in finely shredded coconut or cocoa powder.

Notes: *You can store the chocolate pomegranate truffles in the fridge in an air-tight container for a maximum of three days.*

PART III

Chapter 1: Anxiety, The Monster Within

"I know what it's like to be afraid of your own mind."
- Dr. Reid from Criminal Minds

- Obsessing over small worries that constantly distract you
- Whirling from action to action to try to quiet your minds' nagging
- Attempting to drown out anxious thoughts in any way possible, solemnly wishing they would just disappear

If you are here with us today, you are likely living through all the above and more, trying strategy after strategy to eliminate these causes of stress. Or, perhaps you are seeking help for a loved one that has anxiety that is weighing them down. Or, maybe you are simply here to feed your curiosity of what anxiety is and how it plagues the mind. No matter, I work with anxiety every day and have spent the majority of my existence on Earth immersed in it.

My grandfather was such a worrier that he physically shook, *constantly*. His body would tremble from the overwhelming magnitude of worry that lurked within him. He was a burly southern man who favored anything outdoors and fishing. His long, curly locks framed his rounded face with an always generous smile. When he was at his warmest, he was a magnet to others. However, his most natural state was when he was in worry mode.

What did he worry about? Anything and everything. He was worried about all the typical things that grandparents do; along with I'm sure many countless unspoken things.

"Do you have enough to eat?"
"Do you need the salt or pepper?"
"Are you comfortable? Too hot? Too cold?"

Even though he was a burly man, his voice was soft, so anyone listening had to lean in. I think he like the intimacy it afforded. Whenever we were all at ease, he was at ease.

Us grandkids always ran with the joke, *"Grampy, can we pass you the salt and pepper?"* His anxiousness would disappear with a smile and flush of embarrassment. We did this to show our appreciation, to relieve the tension and let him know he was never a burden and that we loved our big burly gramps for who he was.

Our gramps was a people-person, always curious and invested in others. I have very clear memories of coming home and hearing his low but small voice in the answering machine, *"Hello, it is just me again. Just checking in to see how you are coming along..."*

He needed that regular assurance that everything was, in fact, alright and always preferred to hear it firsthand. And if he could do things for someone, that was even better.

As Gramps aged, his anxiety escalated and he became less able to use it in a constructive manner. There were less and fewer ways for him to release his anxious feelings, to the point he became crippled with worried on a daily basis. When I search into where my own anxiety stemmed from, a picture of Grampy always pops into my mind. When I studied anxiety in graduate school, his shaking body was a perfect analogy. The more time I spent exposed to the study of anxiety in the human body, I began to understand my grandfather better than he likely understood himself most days. I also realized how persuasive anxiety was throughout our family's history. It was what set the foundation for me to deeply understand how much anxiety affected emotions and behaviors.

Thankfully, no one else in my family shook as much as my grandfather did from anxiety; however, looking back, anxiety was the hub of all the spectrum of extremes my family endured. My mother was motivated by her anxiety, while my father was like a balloon, letting stress and anxious feelings build up until he popped with rage.

While no one in my immediate family was ever diagnosed with an anxiety disorder, I can still imagine that just like so many others, they would have felt the same shameful stigma that comes along with all mental health problems, thinking that something is wrong with them. They were simply noticing things in their lives and felt deeply about them; they just didn't have the tools and knowledge to cope with the overload of information.

Through my years as a psychologist, I have gained a different perspective on anxiety and how it alters thoughts and feelings. I have come to see anxiety as a resource and seek to embrace its value in our everyday lives.

Anxiety derives from the feeling of realizing that something we genuinely care about may be at risk, as well as the arrival of resources that we need in order to protect it. Anxiety prompts us to look closer and pay better attention to messages we receive and helps us to gain the motivation we need to take control of situations. The key to getting back a life driven by anxiety and fear is to take control. This is where I have used my knowledge to help others, in ultimately steering them in a different direction of gaining back their willpower.

How Anxiety Overshadows Everyday Lives

Living in denial, second-guessing your every move, thinking ill thoughts about your future, living in fear of the unknown; all these things can overshadow a person's life and lead to constant anxiety.

If you or a loved one is plagued by anxiety, you have probably endured panic attacks and constant negative nagging in your head on a regular basis or have a phobia of some kind feel ashamed of their "sickness."

Anxiety has the power to make everyday folks feel insane, even though they truly aren't. Just like with all people, some days are better than others, but those who experience symptoms caused by these mental ailments typically have a higher count of bad than good days.

They often feel that they are always under a dark cloud that pours rain, but that rain is not made up of just water. Those drops from the sky above their head are created from startling visions, disturbing logic, feelings of worthlessness and/or hopelessness and looks that they receive from both loved ones and strangers when they truly believe they are in a type of personal crisis or feel as if they are about to be pushed over the edge. This is just a small portion of what it is like to live with anxiety.

What is Anxiety?

Anxiety, in its simplest form, is a bodily reaction to unfamiliar or dangerous environments and scenarios. Everyone has the tendency to get anxious from time to time and feel distressed or uneasy. This happens perhaps before a big game, performing in front of an audience or right before a huge job interview. Feeling anxious is a natural response that our bodies can feel during moments like these. Anxiety gives us the boost we need to be consciously aware and alert to prepare us for certain situations.

Our body's "fight-or-flight" response is under this umbrella of reactions. But imagine feeling like this *all* the time, even during the calmest of moments?

Picture a life where you have issues concentrating on everyday tasks, where you may be frightened to leave the safety of your home when you cannot fall or stay asleep because your mind is in a constant whirlwind of thought? Living with an anxiety disorder is debilitating. That is putting it lightly in some cases.

Causes of Anxiety

Every one of us is unique, which means even common disorders, like anxiety and depression, resonate within each of us differently, as well as why we are living with anxiety, to begin with. There are several key factors that cause anxiety disorders to grow in the mind:

- Chemistry of the brain

- Environmental factors
- Genetics
- How we grew up
- Life events

The factors listed above are the basics that lay the groundwork to potentially be a victim of anxiety, but those below mixed with any of those above could set one up to be someone that is at a higher risk than others in the development of an anxiety disorder:
- Alcohol, prescription medication or drug abuse
- Chemical imbalances in the body and/or brain
- History of anxiety that runs in family bloodlines
- Occurrence of other mental health issues
- Physical, emotional or mental trauma
- Side effects one has on particular medications
- Stress that lasts an extended amount of time

The feelings and thoughts that anxiety promotes within a sufferer create a bubble that creates lonely thoughts and feelings, which is why it is no surprise that anxiety disorders are the most common of mental illnesses with the U.S, with **over 40 million American adults** living with one of these disorders as we speak.
If it is any consolation, you are by no means alone when it comes to feeling the way you do. There is still a lot of research being put into finding out why anxiety plagues so many individuals, its specific causes and why it resonates within individuals in such vast ways.

Signs & Symptoms of Anxiety Disorders

All of us will experience anxiety in our lives; it is a normal response to stressful life events. But as you have learned so far or experienced for yourself, these symptoms can become much larger than the events of stress them and can interfere heavily with a happy, healthy way of life.
Below are the most common symptoms of anxiety:
- **Worrying** that is disproportionate to the events that trigger it and is intrusive, making it challenging to concentrate on everyday tasks.
- **Agitation** that causes fast heartrates, sweaty hands, dry mouth, etc.

- **Restlessness** or feeling on edge with a constant uncomfortable urge to move that won't go away.
- Becoming **easily fatigued**, either in general or after a panic attack.
- **Difficulty focusing** on everyday tasks.
- **Issues retaining short-term memory** which results in a lack of performance in multiple areas of life.
- Becoming **easily irritable** in the day to day life.
- Constantly having **tense muscles** that may even heighten anxious feelings.
- **Issues falling and staying asleep** due to continued disturbances in the sleep cycle.
- **Panic attacks** that produce overwhelming sensations of fear.
- **Avoidance of social situations** due to a fear of being judged, humiliated, or embarrassed.
- **Extreme fears** about very specific situations or objects that are severe enough to interfere with normal functioning.

Understanding Social Anxiety

Imagine at random times, feeling so uncomfortable in particular situations to the point of not being able to process what is happening around you or difficulty breathing. Welcome to the life of those that deal with social anxiety. Social anxiety is classified by a major discomfort with social interactions as well as a fear of judgment. There are more than 15 million Americans that deal with this in their everyday lives that struggle with the awkwardness of social settings.

Symptoms of Social Anxiety

The main symptoms of this form of anxiety are feeling intensely anxious when in social situations or avoiding them altogether. Many sufferers have a constant feeling that 'something just isn't right', but are never able to pinpoint it.
As you can imagine, these people have a twisted way of thinking that includes false beliefs of situations and negative opinions from others. Many people fear the interaction days or weeks before the event, which means that social anxiety can manifest in other physical symptoms, such as:

- Sweating
- Shaking
- Diarrhea
- Upset stomach
- Muscle tension
- Blushing
- Confusion
- Pounding of heart
- Panic attacks

The key aspect of social anxiety to remember is that even though these folks have a fear of speaking or interacting with others, it doesn't mean they have nothing to say.

Below are things that those who suffer from social anxiety would say to others to help them understand how they feel:

"I do not want this and I cannot help it. It is not just a bit of nervousness that comes and goes. It is constant stress and living in a world that you start to not recognize."

"In my ability to speak right, I lack confidence. There are many times I want to say something, but hold back because I am afraid of how dumb it may sound or that I will be misunderstood. I am afraid of speaking in groups, phone calls, and approaching people the most."

"I am terrified of people's reactions when I do scrounge up the courage to finally speak."

"My anxiety socially is not a constant. There are certain situations that cause me more anxiety than others. It is a fluid disease."

"Many times, people don't realize that those with this anxiety disorder are suffering because of the lack of physical symptoms. Just because you cannot tell there is something wrong, doesn't mean there isn't."

"I cannot help how ridiculous it may seem."

"It hurts to know that people take my anxiety personally instead of just helping me out."

"I wish I had a social life, but my anxiety won't let me; I am not anti-social."

"It may look like I am zoning out from time to time, but I am actually practicing positive self-talk and breathing techniques to stay calm and ward off a panic attack."

"I am not trying to be standoffish, rude, or snobby, even though it may seem that way when I refuse hugs or don't wish to speak. I simply get overwhelmed and overstimulated easily. All I ask for is respect."

"I want people to break the ice and speak to me first. I am genuinely a nice person, I just

have a fear I am unable to control."

"I wish more people understood that when I say I cannot come, it is because the situation I was invited to feels 'impossible', not because I don't feel like it."

"When I leave early, I am not being disrespectful. I just need to fight off a meltdown with some alone time."

"Social anxiety is not 'shyness'; that is like comparing a stab wound to a paper cut."

No one experiences social anxiety in the same way. Each day is like living a life of constant fear; worrying about the disapproval of others, rejection, not fitting in, etc. They are bound to be anxious to enter or begin a conversation.

Chapter 2: Acknowledging Your Anxiety

While the numbers of those that suffer from anxiety in the United States alone exceed 40 million, you may feel alone in your symptoms as well as what triggers them. Things that set off those anxious thoughts and feelings are a bit different for everyone who experiences anxiety. It is important to take time to focus on yourself and learn what things provide you with peace or create tension in your life.

Common Anxiety Triggers

- The hustle and bustle of everyday life. Life is always busy and there never seems to be time to slow down.
- The inevitable fact that we are only growing older.
- Driving, especially on freeways with many cars or across bridges.
- Not living up to the expectations that we set for ourselves.
- The sense of uncertainty. When we are not on control of situations we tend to freak out a bit. This comes from a lack of communication and anxiety making conclusions for us.
- Ambulance, fire or police sirens.
- Stresses at work – Not performing well enough, not having enough time during the course of the workday to get things done, etc.
- Simply thinking about what triggers your anxiety can be a cause for anxiousness in itself.
- Being too hot is often times directly associated with being claustrophobic.
- The inevitable part of life known as death. This especially goes for individuals who have experienced much loss in their lives.
- Being alone.
- The possibility of finding out that people do not like you as much as you think they do.
- Being judged or verbally attacked.

- Large crowds.
- The inability to predict the future. Those with anxiety often dislike surprises.
- Trying new things.
- Being far away from home or other places familiar to you.
- When many people speak to or at you all at once.
- The struggles that your children may face at school.
- Money! This is a big one. Whether it is saving for a big event such as a wedding or purchasing a home or car, the process of paying monthly bills while still trying to save money for other things.

Getting to the Root Causes of Your Anxiety

What many of us do not realize is that many causes that trigger our anxieties to flare up are actually self-produced. While you can blame your situation, family, friends, etc. for you distress, you are the one who perceives life as it goes on around you. The way you view it, analyze and take it all is all dependent on you. The root reasons behind the curtains of 'Play Anxiety' are usually caused by one of the following reasons.

Negative Self-Talk

It is said by research conducted by behavioral specialists that upwards of 77% of all the things we think to ourselves is quite counterproductive and negative. What we don't realize is that we are being our own worst critic and a detriment to ourselves. Learn to become consciously aware of the way you speak to yourself.
Write down any sort of negative thoughts for a day and then each day forward practice transforming those negative words or thoughts into a happy, loving one towards yourself. While it may feel weird at first, it will become second nature to you once you practice it for a while. Your self-talk is just as important of a daily habit as any other.

Unrealistic Expectations

Sometimes we simply just have too high of expectations that create a high world that we struggle to reach. Expecting those to be perfect and remember all the details about you is just ridiculous. If your expectations fly way above you, you are more than likely missing out on grand opportunities and are unable to truly recognize the good things that are happening that you should be celebrating.

This goes for the expectations you have for yourself as well. Are they actually realistic? If not, how can you go about making them more reasonable and achievable?

The "Should" Thoughts

Do you find your brain thinking that you "should do this" and you "should do that" often? Have you ever just taken a moment to actually find the reasoning behind why you "should"? Telling yourself that you should is equivalent to telling yourself that you are not good enough. It leads to negative self-talk fast and should be avoided. Make a positive list of the things you should do or become. Are they yours or someone else's expectations?

Taking Things Too Personally

Those with anxiety feel like many things that occur are actually their fault when in reality they more than likely had nothing to do with someone's disgruntled behavior or a glare they received. Learn to not take things too personally because you never know what may be happening in the life of other people.

"We are all in the same game, just different levels. Dealing with the same hell, just at different devils." If you think you are the cause of someone's actions, speak up and ask instead of just assuming. This will get rid of a lot of assumptions that go into negatively feeding your anxiety.

Our minds are wired to believe the things that we tell it the most. If we are always engaging in negative self-talk, expect too much of others or ourselves, do things we just merely think we "should" do or worry about those around you, your brain will act negatively as well. It is all about building a positive foundation for your frame of mind for all those thoughts of yours to dwell in. In order to unlock the door to happiness and less stress and/or anxiety, it is time to get thinking in a happy manner!

Pinpointing Your Anxiety

While you can take all the time in the world to read information in regards to relieving anxiety via the internet, books or other media, unless you take action and decide that you truly want to make a change to lower your anxiousness, it will never happen. I am an anxiety sufferer and back just a couple years ago it engulfed my everyday life and drowned me more than a few times.

I finally over time came up with a process that assisted me greatly with determining what triggered my anxious thoughts so that I could get a grip on my life and yield them from continuously taking over my personal life.

- ***Stop*** – When those feeling of anxiousness begin to hit you, stop and take a moment to make a mental note of what you are doing right at that moment. This is easier said than done, for you might be in the middle of a task, conversation, etc. But it is beneficial to take just a moment to identify when you began to feel anxious.

- **Identify** – Recognizing the onset of anxiety will help you come to the conclusion of what actually causes it for you personally. If you develop the capability to notice triggers and feelings when they start to dwell, you can put a stop to them faster. Many people don't realize they are feeling anxious until their symptoms are outrageously taking over them. Over time, you will be able to catch on more quickly what is threatening your happiness and overall well-being.
- **Write** – As you become an expert of taking moments to make mental notes of why you feel anxious, I find that at the end of the day I write down the events during my day, both the goods one and those that triggered my anxiety. I keep a notepad on my cellular device so that I am quickly able to access it to jot down notes at the moment and then write them down on paper before heading to bed. Be sure to write down as many details as possible – what you are thinking, experiencing and feeling, etc.
- **Analyze** – At the end of the week is when I choose to review what I have written in my anxiety notebook. You can review it at the end of each day, week or month, but I do not recommend waiting any longer than that. I wait at least a couple days to a week so that I can see the pattern that my thoughts made. When you are aware of these patterns you are better able to focus on the causes of anxiety and avoid them.
- **Possibilities** – There are numerous things that you can make the scapegoat when it comes to feeling anxious. If you have adequate knowledge of these ideas, you can review patterns and conquer anxiety. Anxiety in many cases is situational. If you are anxious being in

unfamiliar surroundings, expose yourself to these types of circumstances a little time. If your causes are more based on the way you think and view the world, learn to engage in positive self-talk. Once you have a pattern written out, you will be less anxious just by the fact that you have some idea and control over your anxiety situation overall.

Chapter 3: Trauma and Anxiety

The journey of life is exciting, scary, ridiculous, confusing and worth it all at once. But there are times that we all go through some type of emotional distress, whether it be mere sadness, rapid anxiety, addictions to outside influences, obsessions with things or people, compulsions we have a hard time controlling, behaviors that are self-sabotaging, physical injuries, anger, and bleak moods, among the hundreds of other things we go through, think and/or feel.

It is important to learn ways to cope when it comes to hard times, no matter the time frame. Something psychologically downgrading can happen in a matter of mere moments and leave you scarred for the rest of your life. Some people seek out help from other individuals who are professionals at understanding the human mind, but others wish to find help within them. Having the knowledge to help yourself is not an easy feat. It may be easy to read pages upon pages of books and self-help websites that provide information, but it is much harder to put those words into actions.

The world is a much different place now than it was just a decade or two ago. Technology has advanced so rapidly that some of us are overwhelmed with it all, especially the consequences that we receive, whether from our own actions or that of another being who acted upon a current mood. Human beings are not the robots that we seem to want to create so badly these days. We are emotionally driven individuals with a lack of having the knack to help ourselves in times of need and/or trouble.

The worst thing about the constant rise of this distress is the fact that there is no one age group or certain targeted individuals that are more likely to go through it. It is happening clear from late grade school levels all the ways into senior living years. Students have much more stress with perpetual levels of testing and pressure to be better. Employees live their hard-earned careers always fighting to make their way up the ladder with not much reward. Older individuals are continuously having their wages and retirement that they worked their entire lives for whisked away.

It is a dog eat dog world out there with a lot of room to make mistakes that can cause even more friction in our personal lives. With the constant pressure to be better than the next, our society has taught us maybe how to be more proficient in terms of getting things done at school or work, but many of us have forgotten the person that is truly important: OURSELVES. If we do not take care of our emotional health, detrimental things can occur. Below are some signs that you may be experiencing emotional distress. Some of the symptoms may surprise you.

Childhood Trauma and Sensitivity to Anxiety

Trauma during childhood can impact our entire lives. According to the Journal of Affective Disorders, children who experience traumatic situations are much more likely to have anxiety and depressions and fall victim to alcohol and drug abuse. The same study found that females are more susceptible than males to develop anxiety, even with the same rates of trauma.

If left untreated, trauma during childhood can have effects that last throughout someone's entire life. They are likely to developmental disorders that branch out to much more than just anxiety as well.

Common Anxiety Disorders Caused by Trauma

Common anxiety disorders that are caused by traumatic events are:
- Panic disorder
- Obsessive Compulsive Disorder (OCD)
- Post-Traumatic Stress Disorder (PTSD)
- Body Dysmorphic Disorder
- Agoraphobia
- Social Phobia(s)

As you can imagine, trauma anytime throughout your life can play a major part in the development of anxiety and other mental disorders in your lifetime.

Chapter 4: Grabbing your life back from anxiety

Now that you have acknowledged that life could be better and have learned how to interpret why you live a life filled with anxiety, it is time to take your life back, pronto! There is a variety of methods we will discuss in this chapter that can help you gain back the confidence you need to live life to the fullest.

Managing Your Emotions

Emotions are a natural human phenomenon. , and are very present in pressing and painful times. Every day we are driven by some force of emotions:
- We take chances because we get excited about new opportunities
- We cry because we are hurting and make sacrifices for those we love

Those are just a couple examples of emotions; they dictate our actions, intentions, and thoughts with authority to our rational minds. Emotions can become a real problem, however, when we act too fast or we act on wrong types of emotions, which cause us to make rash decisions.

Negative emotions, such as bitterness, envy, or rage, are the ones that tend to spiral out of control the most, especially when triggered. It only takes one slip of our emotions to totally screw up the relationships in our lives.

If you have issues controlling your emotions, here are some steps that you can implement into your everyday life that will help you regain rationality, no matter what challenging situation you are facing:

Don't react right away

You are more likely to make mistakes when you react right away to emotional triggers. When reacting right away to these triggers, you are likely to say and do things that you will later regret.

Before acting on emotions, take a deep breath to stabilize your impulses. Breathe deeply for just a couple minutes and you will be able to feel your heart rate return to normal. One you become calmer, remind yourself that feeling this way is just temporary.

Find healthy outlets

Once you have managed your emotions, you need to learn how to release that build up in the healthiest way possible; emotions are something that you should never let bottle up. Talk to someone you trust. Hearing their opinion of the matter can help to broaden your thoughts and regain control.

Many people keep a journal to write down how they feel. Others engage in exercise to discharge their emotions. Others meditate in order to return to their tranquil state. Whatever activity suits you, find it and use it when emotions get high.

Look at the bigger picture

All happenings in our, both bad and good, serves a purpose in our lives. Being able to see past the moment strengthens your wisdom. You may not understand certain circumstances right away, but over time, you will see the bigger picture as the pieces of the puzzle fall into order. Even when in an emotionally upsetting time, trust that there is a reason that you will comprehend in time.

Replace your thoughts

Negatively fueled emotions create negative recurring thoughts that create cycles of negative patterns over time. When confronted with these emotions, force them out of your mind and replace them with more positive thoughts. Visualize the ideal ending playing out or think about someone or something that makes you happy.

Forgive your triggers

Triggers could be the ones you love the most; you're best friend(s), your family, yourself, etc. There will be times that you may feel a sudden wave of rage when people do things that annoy you or a self-loathing feeling when you remember back to the past when you could have done thing differently. The key to managing your emotions is to first, forgive. This allows you to detach from your jealousy, fury, and resentment. As you forgive, you will discover that disassociating yourself from these feelings will do you the best.

Every day we are constantly reminded of how strong and prominent our emotions are and the power they have. We are bound to take the wrong action from time to time and feel the wrong things. To avoid acting out, simply take a few steps back and calm your spirit that is heightened from outside forces. You will be grateful for mastering your emotions when it comes to building and strengthening meaningful relationships.

Using the Power of Mini Habits

Just after Christmas in the days ending 2016, I was reflecting on the year. I realized that I had tons of room to improve but always failed at keeping up with my New Year's resolutions. Instead, I decided that in 2017, I would explore other options.

On the 28th of December, I made the choice that I wanted to get back in shape. Previously, I hardly if ever exercised and had a consistent guilt about it. My goal was a 30-minute workout, realistic, right?

I found myself unmotivated, tired, and the guilt made me feel worthless. It wasn't until a few days later that I came across a small blog article about thinking the opposite of the ideas you are stuck on. The clear opposite of my 30-minute workout goal was chilling on the couch, stuffing my face with junk food, but my brain went to the idea of 'size.'

What if, instead of carrying that guilty feeling around all the time, I just performed one push-up? I know, right? How absurd of me to think that a single push-up would do anything to help me towards my goal.

What I found was a magical secret to unlocking my potential…when I found myself struggling with my bigger goals; I gave in and did a push-up. Since I was already down on the floor, I did a few more. Once I performed a few, my muscles felt warmed up and I decided to attempt a pull-up. As you can imagine, I did several more. And soon, I exercised for entire 30-minutes!

What Are Mini Habits?

Mini habits are just like they sound; you choose a habit you want to change and you shrink them down to stupidly small tasks.

For instance, if you want to start writing at least 1,000 words per day:

- Write 50 words per day

- Read two pages of a book per day

Easy, right? I could accomplish this in 10 to 20 minutes or so. You will find that once you start meeting this daily requirement, you will far exceed them faster than you would imagine.

What is *More* Essential than Your *Habits*?

You might be wondering how you can become more comfortable in your skin and be yourself in a cruel world with these so-called mini habits. Well, think about it; what is more important than the things you do each and every day? NOTHING. Habits are responsible for 45% of how we behave, making up the foundation of who we are and how happy we are in life.

The main reason people fail to change anything in their life, even the aspects they know need to change is because they never instill new habits. Why? Simply because in the past, they have tried to do way too much, all at once. If establishing a new habit requires you to have more willpower than you can muster, you are bound to be unsuccessful. If a habit requires less willpower, you are much more likely to succeed!

Benefits of Mini Habits

There are many additional benefits that come with utilizing mini habits in your everyday life. Here are a few:
- Consistent success breeds more success
- No more guilt
- Stronger productivity
- Formation of more positively impactful habits
- Generation of motivation

Chapter 5: Belittle anxiety with personal empowerment

Having a negative attitude towards life keeps us from being happy and impacts those that we interact daily with. Science has more than enough proof to show how being positive impacts your levels of happiness and terms of success. This is why making positivity a habit with the help of small changes can help you to drastically change your overall life and the mindset you have towards the world. The life you are living is a direct reflection of your overall attitude. It can be quite easy, almost too easy, to be cynical at the world and see it as a mess of injustice and tragedy, especially thanks to the media that we all spend many hours a day on.

Negativity is holding you back from really enjoying your life and has a great impact on your environment as well. The energy that people bring to the table, including you, is very contagious. One of the best things you can do in your life that is free of charge and simplistic is to offer your positive attitude. This is especially beneficial in a world that loves and craves negativity.

One of my favorite quotes of all time comes directly from the King of Pop, Michael Jackson: *"If you want to make the world a better place, take a look at yourself and make a change."*

As humans, we are creatures of habit. In this chapter, we will outline small but significant changes that can be made to form positive habits that can drastically change the overall mindset of your life around.

Smile

When asked who we think about most of the time, the most honest answer would probably have to be ourselves, right? This is natural, so don't feel guilty! It is good to hold ourselves accountable and take responsibility for ourselves. But I want to challenge you to put yourself aside for at least one moment per day (I recommend striving for more) and make another person smile.

Think about making someone else happy and that warm feeling you get when you receive happiness. We don't realize how intense the impact of making someone smile can have on those around us. Plus, smiling costs nothing and positively works your facial muscles!

Focus on solutions, not problems

Embracing positivity doesn't mean you need to avoid issues, but rather it is learning how to reconstruct the way you criticize. Those that are positive create criticisms with the idea to improve something. If you are just going to point out the issues with people and in situations, then you should learn to place that effort instead into suggesting possible solutions. You will find that pointing out solutions makes everyone feel more positive than pointing out flaws.

Notice the rise, not just the downfall

Many of us are negative just by the simple fact that we dwell too much on the hate and violence that is in our daily media. But what we fail to notice is those that are rising up, showing compassion, and giving love to others. Those are the stories you should engulf yourself in. When you able to find modern-day heroes in everyday life, you naturally feel more hopeful, even in tough times.

Just breathe

Our emotions are connected to the way we breathe. Think about a time that you held your breath when you were in deep concentration or when you are upset or anxious. Our breath is dependent on how we feel, which means it also has the power to change our emotions too!

Fend off other's negativity

I'm sure you have gone to work cheerful and excited to take on the day ahead, but then your co-worker ruins that happy-go-lucky mood of yours with their complaints about every little thing, from the weather to other employees, to their weekend, etc.
It is natural to find yourself agreeing to what others are saying, especially if you like to avoid conflict. But you are initially allowing yourself to drown in their pool of negative emotions. Don't fall into this trap.
Conflict may arise, but I challenge you to not validate the complaints of a friend, family member, or co-worker next time they are going about on a complaint-spree. They are less likely to be negative in the future if they have fewer people to complain to.

Switch the "*I have to*" mindset with "*I get to*"

I am sure you often fail to notice how many times we tell ourselves that we have to go and do something.
- "I have to go to work."
- "I have to go to the store."
- "I have to pay rent."
- "I have to mow the lawn."

You get the picture. But watch what happens when you swap the word have

with the word get.
- "I get to go to work."
- "I get to go to the store."
- "I get to pay rent."
- "I get to mow the lawn."

See the change in attitude there? It goes from needing to fulfill those obligations to be grateful that you have those things to do in your life. This means:
- You have a job to go to
- You have enough money to support yourself and your family to provide a healthy meal
- You have a roof over your head
- You have a nice yard

When you make this simple change, you will begin to feel the warmth of happiness snuggle you like the cold blanket of stress falls away.

Describe your life positively

The choice of vocabulary we use has much more power over our lives than we realize. How you discuss your life is essential to harnessing positivity since your mind hears what you spew out loud.
When you describe your life as boring, busy, chaotic, and/or mundane, this is exactly how you will continue to perceive it and it will directly affect both your mental and physical health.
Instead, if you describe your life as involved, lively, familiar, simple, etc., you will begin to see changes in your overall perspective and you will find more joy in the way you choose to mold your entire life.

Master rejection

You will need to learn to become good at being rejected. The fact of the matter is, rejection is a skill. Instead of viewing failed interviews and broken hearts as failures, see them as opportunities for practice to ensure you are ready for what is to come next. Even if you try to avoid it, rejection is inevitable. Don't allow it to harden you from the inside out.

Rethink challenges

Stop picturing your life being scattered with dead-end signs and view all your failings as opportunities to re-direct. There are little to no things in life that we have 100-percent control over. When you let uncontrollable experiences take over your life, you will literally turn into mush.
What you can control is the amount of effort you put into things without an ounce of regret doing them! When you are able to have fun taking on challenges, you are embracing adventure and the unknown, which allows you much more room to grow, learn and win in the future.

Write in a gratitude journal

There are bound to be days where just one situation can derail the entire day, whether it be an interaction that is not so pleasant or something that happens the night before the day ahead, our mind clings to these negative aspects of the day.
I am sure you have read on multiple sites about how keeping a gratitude journal is beneficial. If you are anything like me, I thought this was total rubbish that is until I started doing it. I challenged myself to write down at least five things that I was truly grateful for each and every day. Scientifically, expressing gratitude is linked to happiness and reducing stress.
I challenge you to begin jotting down things you appreciate and are grateful for each day. Even on terrible days, there is something to be blessed about!

Chapter 6: Everyday techniques to fend off anxiety

Despite the toll that anxiety and its symptoms can have on everyday life and fulfillment, in today's world there are many different techniques and methods you can learn to incorporate into your everyday routine that help you to control and possibly even eliminate anxiety from your life. Each section of this chapter will be dedicated to a specific genre of techniques that anyone has the ability to learn!

Visualization and Anxiety

Seeing *is* believing, which is a key secret to how entrepreneurs and well-known people in society stand out and achieve success and fulfill their dreams. ***Visualization is the simple use of imagination through mental imagery to help form visions of what we want in our lives and how we can make them a reality.***
There are two main kinds of visualization:
Pragmatic Visualization represents a set of days that helps to gain new ideas and interpret what it says/means to them. It helps those understand structures that lie within a set of data.
Artistic Visualization is similar to pragmatic in that it utilizes visuals to convey information but in a different sense. It is used to show people that data is being monitored carefully and shows particular aspects of data that is connected to one another to depict an entire idea.
So, how does learning about these two kinds of visualization help you in your quest to decrease anxiety? Well, visual techniques help to drastically overcome symptoms of anxiety. When the two types are combined, visualization is powerful in obtaining and staying in a calmer state of mind.
When it comes to anxiety, visualization requires one to picture themselves in a safe, peaceful and/or tranquil environment. Anywhere that makes you happier is where you should be imagining yourself during visualization exercises. It does sound pretty funny at first glance, but trust me when I say there is something about being able to transport your mind to somewhere mentally tranquil. Not only will your mind thank you but your body will too, for it becomes much more relaxed and stress-free when performing these practices. Visualization gives people something to distract themselves from the current world that surrounds them.

Why You Should Be Using Visualization

Beyond visualization itself, you can literally view the best of life from the comfort of your own couch. This chapter will showcase the benefits that come with the dedicated practice of learning and incorporating ways of visualization into your everyday life.

- **Improved quality of relationships** – The positive outcomes of utilizing visualization doesn't just end within yourself. Since you are developing a better mindset that aids in your views and beliefs, those around you will like and appreciate the more confident, positive you!

- **Boosts your mood** – When one practices the methods of visualization, they naturally experience a sort of joy that is quite unexplainable to some. Once you finish one of these sessions successfully, you will more than likely feel boastfully happy, calm and relaxed.

- **Relieves stress** – Practicing the ways of visualization naturally causes one to be able to relax. It has a way of quieting the mind to be able to think happier, more positive thoughts which tone down loads of stress that pile on our shoulders almost on a daily basis.

- **Strengthens the immune system** – Thanks to all that dialing down of stress and things that fuel stress, your body is better able to fight off sickness which makes you physically better, longer. This also helps in aiding anxiety because you are not constantly worrying about getting ill all the time as well.

- **Ability to learn new things quicker** – When the mind is in a calmer state, it is able to pick up and grasp new concepts much easier than when it is bogged down with so many negative thoughts and emotions.

- **Able to cope with the feeling of nervousness** – When you take time out of your day to practice visualization, you are initially settling all those negative feelings that you may have about yourself and what others may think of you as well. This immensely helps individuals who are naturally more nervous combat that feeling, which leaves room to try and experiment with new things and ideas. Imagine yourself in a great looking outfit giving that inevitable speech that is due soon. Then imagine an applauding audience. It is quite the confidence booster!

- **Builds stronger concentration skills** – Visualization makes room for your mind to do other tasks efficiently by spring cleaning negative thoughts, feelings, emotions, and past experiences. This doesn't mean it is responsible for getting rid of them 100%, but it helps one to be able to cope and bring down those bad levels to make room for productivity.

- **Assists in overcoming recurring issues** – When the weight of your entire world is upon your shoulders, it is no wonder that we begin to believe that our lives were just made to be a laughing-stalk to some because of how life's unlucky events have left us feeling. This can lead to long-term problems and beliefs. Visualization combats these two things.

- **Can give you a spark of inspiration** – During your sessions, if your mind always veers to one idea in particular, perhaps it is time to take initiative and proceed with the steps in achieving it! Visualizing doing something can directly inspire you to do as such.

- **Makes one more creative** – Visualization not only takes concentration but also a truckload of creativity as well. If you are going to picture something in detail and add the other four senses to that visual, you have to really want to mold it into reality. We all have creative bones in our bodies. Visualization just brings them out more, honing that skill and letting it shine.

- **No boundaries** – As I have mentioned before, when it comes to visualization, practice makes perfect. Just like with any newly acquired skill, one must learn to hone its practice to be able to tweak it when needed and use it to their utmost advantage. With certain visualization techniques, you can literally picture yourself doing something that would otherwise be usually hard to achieve. With those images in mind, you then have a good idea what you must do to actually and realistically accomplish that image you had in your head during a visualization session. This method knows no bounds!

- **Method of practice and rehearsal** – Believe it or not, visualization can be a way to practice your favorite sport or nail that upcoming work pitch that you have been reciting and memorizing for days. Picturing yourself doing or performing something is just as effective as actually completing the task at hand. Utilizing visualization with real, physical practice can get you to honing that skill or memorizing things much quicker.

- **Picture yourself getting stronger and healthier** – Sounds unbelievable, but if you are sick, seeing yourself get better will have the result of getting healthier, sooner. Visualization reduces stress and relaxes your mind, which also assists in healing your body of sickness or physical injury as well. This allows your body to function at its full capacity. You would be surprised what our bodies could accomplish in a day's work if we treated them more like the temples they are and should always be. It is safe to say we take our physical presence for granted most days. And it tends to show more often than not!

- **Gives us joy** – Many people who practice the ways of visualization tend to picture something that brings them happiness. We almost are never quite in the right place or time in our lives to always have what we want and that is okay! But that doesn't mean we shouldn't get the luxury of seeing it for ourselves, right? Picturing a goal or what we want the most from life can bring us quite a load of temporary happiness if one wants to view it that way. Why temporary? If you can picture it, you can eventually and more than likely make it happen in your future, which is why visualization can be a great motivator.

Aspects of Successful Visualization Practices

There are three aspects to successfully become one with visualization:

- **Practice** – Learning the ways of visualization may actually be more stressful and frustrating for beginners because it is not a practice we are naturally keen to perform. Those that start practicing visualization have a false sense of what the experience is supposed to feel like and have false expectations about the outcome. This inhibits the practice from really taking effect. Visualization is something that has to be practiced daily to work for you long-term. If practiced the right way, it will eventually become second nature to you but only if you really dedicate yourself to learning its ways and practicing it every day until you have it down pat.

- **Utilizes ALL the senses** – Visualization doesn't just use your sense of how a certain peaceful place appears to you in your mind. You have to imagine what your safe space smells, tastes sounds and feels like as well. The more detailed you are in regards to your senses, the better visualization you will have and the more relaxed you can potentially become.

- **Actions** – All human beings experience mental barriers that keep them from being happy and the process of practicing and performing visualization is not excluded from this. Even for visualizing experts, bad thoughts from the course of one's day can inhibit one from getting a clear vision of their safe haven. You have to find a way to release and/or transform those bad thoughts and feelings into something that you can tangibly get rid of.

Forms of Visualization for Anxiety

Visualization is a skill that can be utilized to obtain a better life, especially for those that suffer from an anxiety disorder. Now, we will talk about techniques in the visualization world. Although all of these are not for everyone, try them out and see what works for you.

Meditation

Meditation is a superb form of apathetic visualization that can lead to very powerful results. Visualizing through means of meditation is more of an outgrowth than the main focus. When you begin to incorporate meditation sessions into your everyday routine, you will gradually be opening the door to your inner self, which will then lead you to be able to visualize more clearly and easily.

The more experience you have with meditation, the smoother sessions become and the more you get to see and take away from your visions. It is important not to become frustrated with yourself or discouraged from continuing to practice meditation if you are just starting out.

The whole point of meditation is to empty your brain of thoughts and feelings and to let your mind wander to wherever it wants to go. A vital component of meditation is breathing. Learn to focus on how you take in and let out breaths of air. Let your mind veer off to wherever its little heart desires. Once you begin to practice this technique more often, it will become easier and faster to exhaust your mind of concerns or other worries and let other things come in and explore. It will become second nature for you to sit down, relax and get into a clear state of mind so that you can visualize to your contentment.

Meditation makes way for things that you never thought were actually within you. Once you rid your brainwaves of all that noise from the course of your day, thoughts occur at their own pace.

Altered Memory Visualization

This visualization technique targets past memories and learning how to change them to a more positive standpoint. For those with anxiety about things that stem from their past, this is especially helpful in obtaining a brighter state of mind. This technique is one to utilize if you are one that holds on to past anger and resentment from particular situations that you finally want to rid yourself of.

No one can change the past, but you can teach your brain how it views these past scenarios in your mind. Get into a calmed state and visualize the scenario that you wish had a different outcome. Restore things said that were fueled by anger with comments that are controlled and peaceful. This does take some time and you may have to revisit this scene in your head multiple times to nail the outcome that you wish had resulted from the past situation. It is recommended to not do this day upon day in a row, but rather space out revisiting the scene.

Over time, your brain will begin to only recall what YOU have recreated, making a once painful or uncomfortable situation fade away in memory. Try to imagine little cubicle offices in each major section of your brain. In this instance, I like to picture a little office guy that is in charge of just the bad memories. During these sessions, you are instructing him on how to rewrite particular events that have occurred in the past and once they are rewritten the way you once anticipated them to play out, this office dude can start to shred your memories of these occurrences.

Receptive Visualization

This technique is much like viewing a movie inside your head, but you are the director of the scenes within this movie. Get yourself to a quiet space, lie back, get comfortable and close your eyes. Focus on building the scene in which you want to see acted out in your mind.

Once a clear backdrop and scenery is within your mind, place people, noises, smells and sounds within your scene of this movie. It is best to slowly build your way up to the actual scene until you are comfortable and content with it, then it is time for action! Focus on feeling involved within this scene of your "movie."

Treasure Map

This visualization technique not only uses mental fundamentals but also physical components as well. You will need to have an idea of what you want to visualize before getting to the nitty-gritty of performing this method. Start by using your art skills to draw out some type of physical representation of the components you need to achieve in order to reach your ultimate goal.

For example, perhaps you have an upcoming test that you want to get a great grade on. Draw out a building symbolizes a school, a book that you will need to use to study for this test and then a representation of yourself. Try to make your drawing detailed, but do not worry about the maturity of your art abilities too much here. It is not the drawings themselves that are important, but rather what you are imagining WHILE sketching them out.

As you draw out your "map to success", your mind is actually visualizing ways that will get you to where you want to be. Patience is a key with this particular technique, for it does take a bit of time to truly become completely mentally occupied in this exercise. It is crucial to take your notepad and pen to a quiet space and to not be around anything distracting such as a radio, television, people or phones.

How to Design Your Own "Safe Space"

Safe places or spaces are a mind's sanctuary, created for the purpose of retreat if one needs a mental location to be able to visualize or hone their meditative state and reduce stress. Creating one of these is kind of like personalizing a physical space in your home. You want to do anything to truly make it YOURS.

It can be anything from a room inside an imaginary home, a room in your realistic home that you want to visualize differently, the beach, a comforting outdoorsy area, etc. As you meditate or relax and begin to dive deeper into your imagery or visualization session, this is the place you imagine you want to go. It is anywhere that you wish to return to time after time, so put some effort and thought into where you will always find comfort in mentally retreating to.

- **Brainstorm** – The goal is to develop a place that you feel calm, content and happy within, no matter the reason that you retreat to it. If you have difficulty seeking out such a place, start by looking through art, magazines, books, old photographs, etc. Always lean towards ideas that burst with positivity for you.

  - Are you more apt to feel calmer in an outdoor/natural setting or do you feel better within the walls of some type of structure?

  - Are there pieces of writing such as within books, poems of stories that make you feel at ease?

  - Do you feel more comforted by populated areas or tranquil areas?

- **Think of a time where you felt happy and safe** – Memories are the best areas to seek things that bring joy to you. Think back to memories that you were happy, content, playful, peaceful, etc. Write these down in detail. It could be literally anywhere, as long as it brought contentment to you.

- Where did this memory occur?
- How old were you?
- Why did this memory make you happy?
- Who was with you within this memory?

- **Create various rooms** – Your safe space does not necessarily have to be just 2D, one room vision. It can have various sections, compartments or rooms within it. This allows you to trek to different areas throughout your visualization sessions. This also allows one the ability to be able to compartmentalize issues and deal with them one part at a time.

  - *Fill your space with cherished people* – There are many individuals that would rather be alone while in their safe place, while others prefer the company of their favorite people. Imagine who makes you happy and during the course of a visualization session, imagine greeting them and welcoming them into your safe space. This also goes for people in your life that may have passed away that you miss and wish to see. Having conversations with them and asking for advice could make a world of difference!

  - *Utilize ALL your senses* – Seeing is believing, but visions of your safe place are a lot more believable and turn in better results if you learn to engage all your senses while within them. Engulf yourself in tastes, sounds smells and how things feel between your fingers and toes and against your skin. It will enhance your visualization experience ten-fold.

- *Write out all the details* – Once you have taken the dedicated time to develop and build your safe place, write down all the tiniest details that you can remember. Writing in a lot of detail can assist you in returning to that place in your mind easier and more efficiently. Some individuals even videotape, sculpt, draw or paint out their descriptions for safekeeping for future use.

    - Are there animals or people?
    - What do you feel?
    - How small or big is your space?
    - What colors?
    - What surrounds you?
    - What is the ultimate backdrop or setting?

- **Visualize positive results** – The main rule of thumb for visualization is imagining situations acted out in positive manners. This involves a heavy amount of thinking happily and setting up a content scene. Imaging positive outcomes are really just a more in-depth version of regular run-of-the-mill positive thinking.

Developing Anxiety Routines

Anxiety routines are any type of daily routine that you use to calm yourself down in stressful situations and that leaves you feeling physical, mental or emotionally distressed. These routines are meant to help you bounce back from the depths of your own thoughts and live a life full of more passion and fulfillment.

This means it is very crucial to choose routines that not only suit you but are healthy, too. Life runs smoother when you have a routine to fulfill those nasty little voices in your head or when you feel like you may make a bad choice because of your anxiety symptoms. Sadly, some people choose unhealthy habitual routines that not only push them back into a negative state but may even provoke symptoms of anxiety and make them worse.

These bad routines could be anything from drug use, both illegal and prescription, large consumption of alcohol or heavy smoking of cigarettes, etc. You get the picture. Creating an anxiety routine for yourself should not include things that will cause you greater harm in the long run. Honestly, habits like those stated above are only going to make your symptoms worse.

As human beings, we are automatically wired to detect any sort of negative energy that may cause us harm. Anxiety becomes so bad within certain people simply because our bodies do not quite know the difference between stressful triggers that are actually harmless to us versus actual, life-threatening aspects that may be sprung upon us.

Our bodies are made to react to protect ourselves. This is why being mentally prepared for the day that lies ahead of you is so crucial, especially for anxiety sufferers. It is important to back up our thoughts with an extra layer of positivity to promote a sense of safety and well-being. This is much easier said than done, especially when life may not have been a very good friend to you as of late. But being able to mentally develop a positive sense of self is the first step in creating daily routines that help pave your way to a successful life to live and your future.

Routines to Decrease Anxiety

With the right amount of inspiration, the first day or two of adding a new routine to your life can be exciting. You know you are making a positive change that will hopefully help you feel better about yourself and the life you live. However, self-care routines can be a hard thing to manage and utilize on a regular basis once the newness of acting upon it wears off.

Anxiety can leave some sufferers so dismayed by anxious or sad thoughts that they want nothing more than to do away with anything that resonates positive energy. But this is the exact opposite of fighting for yourself and your happiness. Everyone has their bad days and moments and by all means, you are allowed to have and live those. But it is important not to stay tucked away in them for long periods of time.

Developing and executing specific daily routines that you are comfortable with gives those a step by step plan for the day and keeps you prepared for situations or other anxiety triggers from leaping out and mugging you of your happiness. Routines, kind of like exercise, are things we practice daily to keep us in shape, but anxious routines keep our minds in check. You never know when something will catch you off guard, when a person may ask you something that is bothersome or when a debilitating symptom of anxiety will hit you throughout the course of the day. It is better to be prepared than not to be, right?

The Importance of a Balanced Morning Routine

Many functions within routines do them absolutely no good. When the alarm goes off, they tend to hit snooze a few times. When they finally decide to open their eyes, they automatically reach for their phones and look at updates on social media. Many people are already let down by the fact no one messaged them or liked their posts throughout the night.

When their feet finally touch the floor to stand up out of bed, they are already on a path to a negative, self-destructing day. They take a quick shower, down a bowl of cereal and chug a cup of coffee and get to their day job...what is the point?

This lack of routine is non-beneficial. We see our unstructured lives as having no real purpose, which results in a lack of inner peace. We are destroying our happiness without realizing it!

Benefits of a Morning Routine

Creating a morning routine is not only a big part in relieving anxiety, but it also boosts productivity, brings out your inner positivity, helps you to develop and successfully sustain good relationships, as well as being a big reducer of negativities. Morning routines alone have been shown to be the best strategy for reducing stress and relieving those pesky symptoms of anxiety, no matter how long they have resided within you.

Morning routines keep you consciously aware and more grounded throughout the day. In fact, many who were once stubborn and did not want to incorporate a daily routine were eventually surprised at how much better they felt each and every morning. Anxiety levels dropped and confidence and happiness levels substantially rose. A morning routine can literally reduce your anxiety by as much as sixty percent!

Steps to Include in Your Morning Routine

When you **wake up earlier**, you know that you have plenty of time to get up and get ready for your day, which aids in decreased stress levels. If there is adrenaline pumping throughout your body as you rush around to head out the door, it sticks with you for the rest of the day.

Sounds like a waste of time, but **making your bed each morning** is a powerful task that helps you gain the momentum you need to get pumped for the day ahead. For those that suffer from anxiety and depression, making the bed is simple but can make a huge difference because you know you have completed *one* task if not anything else.

Meditation and prayer is a subject with many critics. People view meditation as an act performed only by spiritual individuals. Practicing mindfulness daily has positive side effects that can trigger feel-good hormones in the brains that aid in reducing levels of stress, anxiety and even depression.

Mixing meditation and prayer within your morning routine can be quite vitalizing, giving clarity to your life and your decisions. If you wish to learn more about the power behind the act of prayer, it will be covered in the following chapter The Empowerment of Prayer.

Taking an ice cold shower in the mornings has been proven to provide the human body with a great number of benefits. Cold exposure, also known as cold shower therapy, is nothing new. Our ancestors utilized it as a remedy to treat mental ailments. Showering in cold water provides the body with adequate circulation and tones the skin nicely.

The cold feeling kicks positive responses throughout the body into overdrive. It accelerates the repairing of cells, which reduces inflammation, pain, and speeds up our metabolic processes. The icy waters help lower negative levels that depression and anxiety can hover over us. Standing under the cold water for just a couple minutes can yield you these benefits.

Substitute your breakfast with coffee or tea to bump up energy levels and replace your usual breakfast eats. This is not recommended for absolutely everyone, but if you are trying to find ways to keep hunger away for the first portion of your day, give it a shot!

Learn how to **utilize a journal** to make "morning pages" as part of your routine in the mornings. This is my personal favorite way to "mind dump" any curious or troubling thoughts you had during the previous day and the night before, as well as random ideas that pop into your mind. I write in my journal after taking a shower, since great ideas tend to spring during those few minutes. When you are able to write down all the negative feelings on paper, you can then get through the day with a clearer state of mind.

Practice gratitude by jotting down things you would miss if they were no longer in your life, such as objects, people, etc. into your morning pages.

To start the day on a positive note, **jot down what you are looking forward** to that day. This tells our brains to look up, think up and be bright and helps to relieve anxiety.

Write down your intentions at the beginning of each day, no matter how corny they may sound, such as *"I will choose to be consciously present today."*

Write out important tasks that you wish to achieve during the day to ensure you will feel prepared and have a fulfilling plan. This will ease your mind so that you can develop a clear path of action to achieving that days' goals.

I know I have mentioned writing a lot, but like I said before it is a powerful tool. Every morning our brains are ready to go and on high alert, so it is good to have a well-thought-out plan of action.

Write down at least three to five of the most important tasks that you have to complete. Focus on ones that stress you out just thinking about them. Then, ask yourself the following questions about the tasks you have jotted out so that you can prioritize them accordingly:

- Which tasks will help me inch closer to achieving my main goal?

- What task do I have the most fearful anxious thoughts about?

- Which tasks have the potential to cancel out others if done successfully?

Spend 90 minutes every day working towards accomplishing your priorities. Targeting your main goals during the morning hours help you to get them accomplished productively.

Other Morning Methods to Relieve Anxiety

Play uplifting music to ensure an upbeat, positive mood. Create a playlist to play throughout your morning routine. Make your phone's alarm tone a good song to wake up to. You would be surprised at what a difference this effortless step takes.

Spend time with a pet(s) to help raise your dopamine and serotonin levels, resulting in lessened anxiety and depression. Pets also motivate us to climb out of bed and give us the initiative to take on the day, even when our anxiety tries to get the best of us. Adding them to your morning routine is a bonus for not only you but for your pet's well-being too!

Change your scenery in simple ways; Go outside, take a walk. Visit your favorite café and grab a coffee. Go out with a friend. The longer you dwell in a space that sucks away happiness, the worse you will feel.

Interactions with the outside world can be enough to distract you from your anxious habits. This is another reason routines are so important in aiding anxiety. Avoiding responsibilities can actually damage you mentally more than you realize. It is good to get your attention off the darkness of life that resides inside your head. It only makes your anxiety worse when you sit around and obsess over it.

Coping with anxiety and its symptoms can lead to a life of great discomfort. Having some type of structure in the form of routines can be quite crucial to one's success in living a happy, go-lucky life. The next few chapters will cover other types of routines in detail that can help relieve and maybe even make your symptoms disappear for good! It is all about you to initiate making the change.

Chapter 7: Transforming Your anxiety for a better life

If you are feeling anxious or depressed about your future and are allowing negative thoughts to get the best of you and dampen your motivation for success, then learning to use anxiety to your advantage is a must.

Personally, I have learned to *choose* to view my anxiety has a valuable asset that yields me to lead a more authentic life. I live empathetically, for my anxiety has made me a vulnerable person and thus, helped me deepen my life's relationships.

Having anxiety just means I am not mellow enough to take things for granted in life, therefore, making life a richer experience all the way around. In fact, there are a few inspirational ways that anxiety has helped me to elevate my life:

- Got me actively involved in personal development
- Taught me how to think in the present and act now
- Got me reading more books and discover how it heals the mind
- Started me on tracking my success and not just on failure
- Taught me how to make a positive game out of my life
- Assisted me to take control over my life
- Reconnected me to the habit of learning new things every day
- Showed me the power of meditation and visualization
- Allowed me to see that I am not the only one in my life that suffers from degrees of anxiety
- Has taught me to be a more actively vulnerable person

Using Anxiety to Your Advantage

Believe it or not, anxiety can be used for good and can be a powerful force in motivating yourself to achieve your desires. Using stress to add momentum to your life is constructive, instead of allowing it to deconstruct our lives.

Redefining danger

You must learn to see anxiety differently; anxiety, before our brains get a hold of it and dwell, is just a warning sign used for our survival. At this point, you are allowing anxiety to make you feel panicked. But even when that warning sign lights up, it doesn't mean you are in danger. You must save this energy for when you really need to make quick decisions.

Create a list of less to most dangerous to help identify a good spectrum of threats. With that comparison, you will be able to see what "dangerous" situations are safe and which ones are frightening.

Channel your stress properly

Diamonds don't grow from trees; they are coals that turn into something more beautiful through pressure. Channeling stress positively into energy for motivation does take time and can be physically and emotionally draining. But instead of allowing negative thoughts take hold of you and send you down that same spiraling hole of anxiety, look at the situation before you differently; view it as your time to *shine*! When negativity starts to manifest in your mind, challenge those thoughts. When you challenge them, you will find that the negativity in them is totally empty in the first place.

Stop trying to do your best

There are two kinds of people: those that do their best and those that can *do better*. However, those that strive to do their best constantly are the ones that end up emotionally drained than those who do better. Why? Because when you do your best, you are settling. When you strive to *do better*, you accept that you are not doing as good as you know you can. For anxiety sufferers, what they do isn't good enough for them. They either drown in their shortcomings or have learned to take the opportunity to improve themselves.

In those with anxiety, underestimation is a common cognitive distortion. When we tell ourselves that we can do better, we know how to reject our deficiencies and go out of their way to prove themselves wrong.

Chapter 8: Battling anxiety like a true warrior

"The only thing we have to fear is fear itself."
- *President Theodore Roosevelt*

Marines, SEALs, and Special Forces have no choice but to face life-threatening danger head-on regularly. The fact is, if they do get caught up in fear, they are more likely to lose their lives. While many of us will thankfully never have to face these experiences, why aren't we using the fear-crushing tactics that they use in our own personal lives?

Spend time preparing

If you are worried about a work presentation, stressing over a job interview, or freaking out about the upcoming rap battle that might help you move out of your mom's house, then stop, prepare, and practice instead of sitting around.

The key is to lose yourself in the moment, which you to by devoting a ton of energy into preparing for what you are worried about. Spend 75% preparing and 25% for the actual event.

SEALs are able to erase fear by practicing upcoming mission until they feel naturally confident. When the unknown becomes more known to them, they don't have to lie to themselves about the risks, but instead put themselves in a better position to handle the unknown, which develops confidence.

Learn to *manage* fear

One of the best ways to deal with fear is to laugh about it. What? You read that right! Laughter lets you know that things are going to be okay and work out. Don't worry; there is evidence to back this theory up. A study by Stanford University showed that those that were trained to make jokes to respond to negative images. This is a much healthier way to deal with fear. The world is an inevitably twisted place, so seeing the funnier side of things makes it easier to deal with.

Breathe

When your heart is beating from your chest, your joints turn into Jell-O, and sweat is pouring off your face, then the best thing you can do to calm the physical manifestations of fear derived from anxiety is to breathe.

That simple? YES. By just inhaling for four seconds and exhaling for four seconds, SEALs can calm their nervous systems and maintain control of their natural biological responses to fear.

You are essentially bending your body's software to better control the hardware. In other words, you are giving yourself a pretty bomb superpower! Breathing helps the body go from the fight-or-flight response of the sympathetic nervous system to the relaxed response of the parasympathetic nervous system.

Tactical breathing used by Navy SEALS for performance just prior to a tense situation or during a workout:

Breathe through the nose. It's very important to breathe through your nose since breathing through the nose stimulates nerve cells that exist behind sternum near the spine that triggers the parasympathetic nervous system. Anxiety is a sympathetic response and parasympathetic counteracts that. This calms your body, which then calms your mind.

1. Relaxed sitting position and right handle on the belly.
2. Activate the breath by pushing belly out and then inhale deeply for a count of four. Inhale to the belly. This pulls breath deep into the lungs. Exhale through the nose for a count of four, pulling the belly button toward the spine. Repeat this three times.
3. Now breathe in through belly and diaphragm for a count of four, again inhaling into your belly and this time lifting your chest. Again, exhale for a count of four so that your rib cage falls and your belly button pulls toward your spine. Repeat three times.
4. Next, use the same technique, this time inhaling for a count of four through the belly, diaphragm and your chest, with a slight raise of shoulders for inhaling. Exhale for a count of four three the chest, diaphragm, and then the belly. Repeat three times, eventually working your breaths up to eight counts.

Next, box breathing is a technique used by the U.S. Navy SEALS to maintain focus and to calm nervous system after a tense situation, such as combat, an intense workout or anytime the desire is to center and focus.

Trains for diaphragmic breathing or deep breathing. Relaxes the whole system and provides oxygen to the brain to focus better. Improves energy. It can also be used by you to regain your sense of balance, concentration, and relaxation and can be practiced at any time. Use the same technique as tactical breathing but you use a five-count hold between breaths.

1. Get in a relaxed sitting position
2. Inhale deeply through the nose for five seconds

3. Hold the air in your lungs for five seconds
4. Exhale for five seconds, releasing all the air from your lungs
5. Hold your lungs empty for five seconds
6. Repeat for five minutes, or as long as you feel necessary

Don't keep things bottled up

Fear is just like terrible liquor; it sucks when you drink it and has negative effects that last a long time, which is why it is important to deal with it before and after the fact.

Talking about scary experiences helps soldiers locate the meaning behind it all. This communication allows them to process what they have been through positively and helps them to create closer relationships with their mates. Scared? Admit it to a friend. Hearing it out loud can help you pull it out, confront it, and deal with it.

Overpower that inner nagging voice

We are all aware of the inner chatter that occurs in our mind on a daily basis. In fact, our inner voice can be really negative the majority of the time. Wouldn't it be cool to have an inner monologue that reminds us how confident and awesome we are? Wouldn't it be great to have an inner motivational speaker to get us through tough times?

Well, you can. In times of stress, our brains are wired to create self-talk that can increase our feelings of fear. As a soldier, they are expected to fight against their inner self-talk and focus on positive portions of experiences. With practice, they are easily able to ignore or even erase the negativity their brains are throwing at them. So, you can do the same in your own life.

Fear and anxiety thrive when we imagine the worst. We developed imagination to be able to project into the future so we can plan ahead. However, a side effect of being able to imagine possible positive futures is being able to imagine things going wrong. A bit of this is useful; after all, there really might be muggers or loan sharks. But uncontrolled imagination is a testing ground for anxiety and fear that can spoil otherwise happy lives.

Some people misuse their imagination chronically and so suffer much more anxiety than those who either future-project their imaginations constructively or who don't tend to think about the future much at all. Anxious, chronic worriers tend to misuse their imaginations to the extent that upcoming events feel like catastrophes waiting to happen. No wonder whole lives can be blighted by fear and anxiety.

Think of the worst-case scenario

No matter what you are afraid of, you always have the opportunity to avoid it for the rest of your life. However, soldiers don't get that choice. They face similar situations time and time again that scare them. To ensure fear doesn't overrule them, they simulate stressful scenarios and try to experience the emotions with them as well.

Instead of thinking happy thoughts and ignoring what you are afraid of, start looking at the worst things that can possibly happen. When you are able to picture the worst fear and stay within an emotional experience instead of pushing yourself out of it, your mind tends to get over the fear naturally.

Reframe your mindset

Reframe you definition of symptoms. Reframe the symptoms of anxiety - give them a different meaning. Those sweaty palms, racing heart, and lightheadedness can mean a panic attack or they can mean the most exciting and fun adventure of your life! Your body doesn't know the difference and it is just doing what it does by nature, but you can choose how you define that sudden rush. Don't believe me?

How do you think those adrenaline junkies dives off cliffs, jump motorcycles or swim with sharks? Their definition of what we call fear is definitely different. They still experience the same potent chemicals coursing through their body, but the sensations have a different meaning to them. What you experience as fear, dread and near death can be defined as thrilling, exciting, and aliveness to someone else.

The beautiful thing about consistently and purposely redefining these symptoms is you can actually rewire your brain. This leads us to neuroplasticity.

Neuroplasticity

Neuroplasticity occurs with changes in behavior, thinking, and emotions. With conscious practice, we can alter our neural pathways to move naturally towards our desired emotions, such as being thankful, calm, and happy and away from anger, stress, and panic.

As you choose to respond with positive emotion, you can strengthen the neural pathways to the desired emotions. As you make more neural connections over time to your desired emotion, the pathways to the negative reactions eventually become weaker and scrambled. This even works while using mental rehearsals of the situation and practicing your desired response.

Remember, this can also work in reverse. If you have a habitual response to circumstances, such as being angry in a traffic jam and you repeat these responses over and over in a high state of emotion, you will strengthen the neural pathways towards the emotion of anger in that situation. The masters over the centuries who taught positive thinking and faith may have actually been on to something and now we can prove it scientifically.

Get moving

Exercise is usually associated with weight loss, improved physical health, and a stronger immune system. But the benefits of exercise can expand much more. Exercise is just as important for your mental fitness as it is your physical health. Aerobic activity promotes the release of endorphins that are released in the brain and act as painkillers, which also help to increase a sense of well-being. Endorphins also improve energy levels, provide a better night's sleep, elevate your mood and provide anti-anxiety effects. Exercise also takes your mind off of your worries and breaks the cycle of negative thoughts that contribute to anxiety.

It is recommended to perform 30 minutes or more of exercise five days a week to have a significant impact on anxiety symptoms. You don't need a formal exercise program at the gym to experience these benefits. Light physical activity has been shown to have the same effects, including gardening, housework, washing the car and walking around the block. These can be done in small intervals throughout the day.

It's more important to do some sort of physical activity on a consistent basis than to aim for something that is not sustainable. Be realistic and if you need to start with smaller goals, do so. This is all about taking care of yourself in a way that works for you.

The single, most important natural tool you can use to beat anxiety is regular exercise. It sounds cliché, but the truth is that exercise affects the mind and body in ways that science is still discovering.

There is a reason that anxiety prevalence has grown with our increasingly inactive lifestyles. Jogging every day can make a world of difference in how you deal with stress, how your anxiety symptoms manifest, and how you regulate your mood.

The best methods of exercise to combat anxiety are:

- **Running** releases feel-good hormones that have exponential mental health benefits. It can help you fall asleep faster, improve memory, lower stress levels, and protects against developing depression.

- **Hiking** in a wooded or hilly location has natural calming effects on the brain. Being around plants and Earthly sights helps to reduce anxiety thanks to the chemicals plants emit. Plus, being out in nature is great for your health and memory function.

- **Yoga,** a lot like meditation, has been found to significantly reduce anxiety and other neurotic symptoms that can lead to irritability and depression. It not only strengthens your core but helps you to focus on breathing, which is the key to relaxing the mind and combating anxiety.

Chapter 9: Rediscovering yourself after hurricane anxiety

Those that live with and through the darkness of anxiety can find themselves waking up each day unhappy. Life is short and there comes a time where re-evaluating your life in order to revamp parts of it to ensure your happiness and fulfillment.
We all get lost in life from time to time. We forget old passions we had, give up interest in pursuit of something else, etc. But it is never too late to rediscover what makes you great and what makes you feel truly alive.

When were you the *happiest*?

Take a moment to remember when you were the most content with your life. In high school? College? Before marriage, family, and kids? When you began your family? Started your business? Pursued a new hobby?
No one peaks at the same time or levels in their lives. The key to regaining contentment is not to think of those fond times as "the past", but to figure out how to find that feeling of happiness again where you currently are in your life. How can you re-incorporate those things that brought you joy in the life you are living now?

What makes you *unhappy*?

What makes your blood pressure shoot through the roof? Figuring out the things that push your last buttons is just as important as knowing what helps you keep a positive outlook. When you are able to clearly point out the toxic influences, you will be better able to erase them and develop better, healthier ways of living. We tend to hold onto things from the past that has negative impacts on our current lives. What grudges are you holding onto? These are toxic and are keeping you from being your best self! No matter what it is, from a toxic ex-partner to a job that drains you, cutting these negative influences will allow you ample space to grow in a positive direction.

Write!

When negative thoughts are constantly bouncing around the brain, it can be very easy to become overwhelmed. We tend to forget how much our daily thoughts impact our lives. They take hold of our power, telling us who we are and what are and aren't capable of. We are the only ones that have the power to take action to erase pesky thoughts from inhibiting our success in life.
I have found that organizing thoughts by writing them down makes them more

abstract. When you can visualize them on paper, it makes them concrete.
Write out a list of pros and cons, random thoughts that pop up, poetry, grocery lists, anything that comes to mind. All writing can be therapeutic and helps us to rediscover how our voice sounds, which radiates who. I challenge to find yourself again with the power of good old pen and paper.

Learning to Love Yourself Again

To rediscover yourself, you need to learn how to love yourself again for who you are, and all parts of yourself, including your flaws and everything you have endured. There are millions of places that offer up 'good advice' to practice self-love, but they never explain exactly how to do so.
Loving yourself is a vital piece of the puzzle when it comes to positive personal growth. It allows us to fulfill our dreams and create happy and healthy relationships with others too.

Care about yourself as much as you care about others

This sounds almost too simple, but many of us are not selfish enough when it comes to fulfilling our wants and needs. It is hard to remember that you are *not* selfish when it comes to caring about yourself and your wellbeing.
Showing yourself compassion shows those in your life that you are able to take care of yourself. No one can pour from an empty pot, which means you need to take care of yourself in order to take care of others in your life. Treat yourself the way you treat your best friend, with caring, concern, and gentleness, no matter what is happening in your life.

Maintain boundaries

Jot down a list of things you need emotionally, both what is important to you and what upsets you. The list can be made up of anything, from wanting sympathy to being celebrated, to being cared for, etc. Whatever is important to you, no matter how silly it sounds, **Write. It. Down.**
We can often find ourselves smack dab in the middle of the confusing conflict and wonder how we got there in the first place. We ask ourselves how we attracted this situation and the people in it with us. While you still need to take responsibility for your actions, it is also crucial to not fall into a pit of self-blame that can cause stress, but rather really look into what is occurring. Many people lack inner confidence and have no idea what they are worth. This lack can leave us living in a sum-zero equation; we are loved completely or become completely unlovable.
I have found from my psychological studies and personal experiences that there are two very simple questions to help anyone restore healthy boundaries in their

life to live a dignified life:

What does this situation negatively represent about yourself? How are you tolerating situations and the behaviors of those around you reinforces your low-worth within you? Those in our lives are a mirror of our own biases, hopes, and fears. *"All anger stems from anger at the self."*

What is your worst fear about saying "no"? Have you ever been left with the thought of you are a bad person because someone's behavior has left you feeling guilty? Well, stop! Challenge that thought by thinking about other situations you have been through. When that happens, the thought that you are a "bad person" falls apart. What matters, in the end, is simple math: people will either *add* or *subtract* to your life.

So, what have you written? The things you write are what you should consider your personal boundaries. When someone ignores something on that list, you should consider it as them crossing boundaries that you have respectively set for yourself. Do not ignore how you feel if this happens, for they are there to tell you what is right from wrong.

Inform others about the boundaries you have set for yourself and be forthcoming with what you will and will not tolerate. When you are assertive with your boundaries, this plays an important part in building a positive self-esteem and allows you many opportunities to reinforce your beliefs, what you cherish, and what you deserve from life.

Do YOU?

Take the time for yourself to establish the things that make you feel good about yourself and about your life as a whole, no matter what it is. Just learn to be aware of how you feel when you go about acting on certain things. For example:

- Are you exhausted by the work you do, but feel thrilled when gardening?
- Are you joyful when reading out loud to your children?
- Do you feel a sense of fulfillment when you write poetry or volunteer in your community?

Once you figure out what makes you feel good about yourself, make those things a priority by implementing them into your every day or weekly schedule. No matter what makes sure you go out and do them! This may mean you have to give up other things to make time for them, but it also means that you may need to re-evaluate your schedule and life more so that you are doing what you honestly enjoy.

To ensure that you are doing these things, there are more than likely going to have to be actions you take to get to those happiness goals, such as saving money to buy supplies to paint, waking up an hour earlier, exercising more, etc.

It is important to realize that you need to do what you need to in order to fulfill your happiness goals. You cannot allow yourself to blame others if you do not fulfill these things. It is time to be a little selfish and fill up your own teapot so that you can fill up the cups of others in your life! This will help you to not only feel better and do better by other people, but it will help you to clear the fog on inconsistent negativity from your life and enable you to truly love yourself and your life once more.

PART IV

Chapter 1: What is CBT?

None of us have control over every aspect of our lives. Therefore, we all must play the hands we are dealt as we navigate through life. Unfortunately, many of the circumstances we have to deal with are unpleasant and can leave us with lasting scars that can start a domino effect of negative thoughts that seem to never end.

It is important to understand that our ability to control many of the elements in our lives is out of our hands; we can't even control the thoughts that seem to flow endlessly through our minds. Still, this does not mean that we are completely helpless. While much of these things happen against our will, there are many things we can do to change the situations we face. At the very least, we can control how we respond to the external events and factors we deal with from day to day. We have the ability to control our reactions to events, thoughts, and internal beliefs about what is happening to us.

This adjusted kind of thinking is at the heart of CBT. It is a research-based approach to a treatment that will address a wide variety of mood and anxiety disorders. A fundamental belief behind CBT is that after experiencing certain situations, certain thoughts are developed in the mind. These thoughts lead to a variety of different feelings (many unpleasant), which can trigger negative reactions. Since feelings are not that easy to change, the concentration of the therapy is on challenging the thoughts that trigger those feelings and once you can control your feelings, you will be able to control your actions. As you develop these new skills, you will be able to manage your life better, which by extension, will allow you to build up a more positive view of the world, and thus have an improved pattern of behavior.

So, rather than pouring out your past to a therapist, opening up painful wounds of the past, and examining every minute detail of them, you and your therapist will work together to discuss the problems you are facing today, set a series of goals, and then apply different strategies and exercises you can apply to help you achieve them.

The Science Behind It

Unlike psychoanalysis, a common form of therapy developed by Sigmund Freud, where treatment is based on early life experiences and uncovering hidden memories that may have been buried, CBT takes an entirely different approach in healing the mind. In CBT, the problems are the foundation for the treatment.

In the early part of the 20th century when psychoanalysis was the accepted form of treatment, you would have spent an endless number of sessions talking about your past. The psychoanalyst would likely interrupt your dialogue with occasional questions about what you might think this image or that person meant, forcing you to think deeper about your reaction to certain events, people, and influences in your life. His goal would have been to get you to explore hidden messages stashed somewhere in your psyche.

At some point, the treatment would gradually take effect and your feelings would start to experience a change. This form of treatment, while effective, would often require a long-term commitment, which could take years to complete, if ever.

About the middle of the 20th century, we began to understand better how the brain worked. Initial research into the function of this organ started focusing on the more recent scientific discoveries relating to both animal behavior and then later in the field of metacognition.

As scientific research progressed over the last century, they have been able to develop a better understanding of learning, behavior, and cognition (our thoughts); it was a natural progression from Freud's form of therapy to what we use now. First, experimenters began to recognize that even animals could associate two separate events together. For example, an experimenter would ring a bell and then give food to a dog. After this action was repeated several times, the dog would automatically associate the bell with food. It was apparent that the dog understood that the sound of the bell meant food.

The next progression was the discovery that helped us understand how human behavior developed. Scientists wanted to understand what would make a person more likely to do one thing and less likely to do another. It was quickly understood that if you punish someone for an action (giving them an unpleasant result), then they would cease the action. The opposite was true with a reward system. If a reward was given, the individual would then be encouraged to continue the action.

This knowledge was quickly applied to mental health where they could now focus their attention on treating the behavior of a patient rather than rehashing all of its past experiences. The patients that are most benefited from this type of therapy are, in a sense, stuck in a certain pattern of behavior. The trigger for that behavior may have happened in his or her childhood or it may have happened in the past few months. The time of the trigger or the real nature of it is not as important as addressing the present state of affairs. The therapy, therefore, is focused on changing that behavior so that he can get out of his rut and start living his life again.

The next evolution of CBT was developed much later in the 60s and 70s. The focus then was on identifying what was really triggering that behavior. It was determined that it was the power of the thoughts and their effect on emotions, which in turn, was triggering the actions. Psychiatrists recognized that to understand how a person feels, they must first understand what a person was really thinking. If a person is struggling with anxiety, then chances are their thoughts were full of thoughts of danger or risk.

Up until that point, they had recognized the cause and effect scenario that was playing out in a person's mind. For example, someone who is afraid of elevators would see the elevator and automatically feel fear.

What they realized later was that there was one missing element that needed to be understood. It wasn't the elevator that was causing the fear in the person, but it was their mind's interpretation of what that elevator actually meant. This goes back to the original premise that what a person thinks is what dictates his emotions and his behavior.

However, we all know that what we think and believe is not always accurate. According to his book *Healing the Addicted Brain,* Dr. Harold Urschel explains that once you begin to analyze your thoughts, you will inevitably find inaccuracies in your reasoning. These inaccuracies tend to reappear over and over again in your mind until corrected. In other words, all of us have distorted thinking and need to be aware of them. In fact, just the simple act of recognizing and acknowledging them will automatically make it easier to change your thought process and help you to replace them with healthier thoughts.

So, if one can get inside the thought process and find the flaw, correcting certain behaviors could be addressed simply by correcting the wrong thoughts that were playing out in their mind at the time. This means that if a person was struggling with irrational thoughts, these could be replaced with more realistic beliefs through a process of challenging them and arming them with a new way of thinking. Analysts were no longer focused on finding the root cause of a problem and could now focus on changing the thoughts that trigger unwanted behaviors.

Through CBT, analysts could help their patients by giving them a set of skills that could be learned, practiced, and through a regular application on their own, could work independently to address their issues.

How it Works

As you read these words, the whole process sounds relatively simple. At first glance, you might have even wondered why a person would need a therapist to figure this out, and you'd be right. But, for those who are stuck in that endless loop of unwanted behavior, it still remains a real challenge.

It is a huge step from Freudian therapy to CBT. A person has to first come to the understanding that three core elements of our human makeup are completely interconnected: our thoughts, feelings, and behaviors. It is literally impossible to change one without changing either of the other two.

This concept can be illustrated simply. If you are struggling with feelings of anxiety, it is usually because your mind is overwhelmed with thoughts of dangers that you want to avoid. However, if your thoughts of danger are distorted, then your reaction to those thoughts will be strange, out of the ordinary, and even extreme. It is only a short step from a fear of danger to trigger our fight-or-flight response, which will either cause us to avoid the situation altogether or to take an aggressive stance.

The Basic Principles of CBT: In order for CBT to be effective, there has to be a good relationship between the therapist and the client. At the very least, there must be a mutual respect for each other and it is extremely important for the therapist to get a good understanding of how the client sees things.

From this area of mutual respect, the foundation for treatment can be laid. After that, there are several other basic principles that must be followed:

- CBT is not an open-ended therapy session – it has a time limit. In most cases, the time with a therapist runs only 10-15 sessions. This puts a slight pressure on the client to not procrastinate in getting started with the specific steps the therapist will give him as homework. He is less likely to put it off until a more convenient time.

- CBT is based on more than a century of research studies. From the beginning, a therapist can give a pretty reasonable estimate as to how long a program can run given the client's unique mental state of mind, and how much of a benefit he can expect to achieve in that time period. As they work together through the sessions, it will be easy to see which parts of the program are working well and which ones are not and make adjustments accordingly.

- CBT always has a very specific objective for the client. It is not about looking at the past but is more about achieving a specific goal. You can't make progress if you don't have a direction to go in, and it won't take long before you will see evidence that the program is helping you to get to the behavior you want to display.

- CBT is a team effort. The therapist doesn't "fix" you. You work together to address and discuss out a certain issue. Each party in the team has something to contribute; the specialist understands just how CBT works, and you (the client) understand how you work. Bringing the two together, as a team, allows both to tailor a treatment that will address the specific needs of the client.

- CBT is well-organized. CBT sessions are not hours of aimless ramblings with a therapist. Instead, they have structured in such a way that the patient knows exactly what his objectives are and the steps they are going to take to get there. The first sessions are dedicated to creating a roadmap outlining every step in the treatment plan. Throughout the program, both the therapist and patient can check to see if they are still on course or if adjustments are needed.

- CBT is about the present. While CBT looks at past events in a patient's life, its primary focus is on what can be done today to fix the problem. It stresses the importance of finding ways to change thoughts and behaviors today so that there can be immediate relief.
- CBT involves action. Both the therapist and the patient are fully engaged in the process. Without a commitment from both parties, it won't be successful. From the very beginning, it requires both to be fully involved with each stage of the treatment.
- CBT focuses on skills. Patients go through each therapy session learning different skills they can continue to use once the session is over. These skills teach you how to identify the mind games you play with yourself, the self-sabotaging strategies you use, and teach you how to stop those bad habits in their tracks and choose healthier and more productive options.
- CBT stresses practice. You have 168 hours in a week and can count on only one hour of time with your therapist. So, in order to get the most out of each session, it is important that you practice each of the strategies learned in your session on your own. The more work is done in between sessions the faster the progress will be.

Changes Thought Patterns and Belief Systems

Since Cognitive Behavioral Therapy is based on the evidence that our ***perceptions*** of the situations in our lives dictate how we feel emotionally, our perceptions of the world are, therefore, the direct result of what we think is really happening or will happen. These are the elements of our lives that need to be adjusted.

For example, an individual may find something in this book and think it is exactly what he is looking for. Because he ***believes*** it is beneficial for him, he then feels good and perhaps even relieved to have found the solution to his problem. However, another person may read the same information and feel entirely different. He may believe that it isn't the right solution for him or that following the exercises are beyond the scope of his ability. As a result, he will feel disappointed and maybe even discouraged at not finding the answer to his problem.

In theory, it is not the experience that causes people to feel the way they do, but it is their perception of the situation or their thoughts about the experience that needs to be modified. We all understand that when a person is under stress, their viewpoint of a situation is often extreme, inaccurate, and unrealistic, so if it is the perception of an experience that triggers negative habits, then this is the area that needs to be focused on.

With CBT, people are helped to identify those negative thoughts, give an honest and realistic appraisal of them, and then learn strategies to help them to readjust their distorted thinking. Once they are able to think more realistically, they will begin to see things differently and it will be easier for them to adjust their behaviors. The therapy works within a narrow focus of solving their immediate problems and making behavioral changes.

Its Purpose – Who it Can Help

Of course, CBT is not a catch-all for all psychological disorders. It has proven to be most effective for the treatment of anxiety, depression, and other forms of mood disorders including obsessive-compulsive disorder, bipolar, and PTSD. While the National Institute for Health and Care Excellence (NICE) specifically recommends CBT for the treatment of anxiety and depression, there are many more mental health issues that it can be very effective with.

Because of its unique flexibility, the therapy can easily be adapted to a wide range of needs. There is a whole list of psychological issues that can be benefited by it including:

- ADD/ADHD
- Alcohol abuse
- Anger management
- Anxiety
- Bipolar disorder
- Borderline personality disorder

- Chronic fatigue syndrome
- Chronic pain
- Depression
- Drug abuse
- Eating disorders
- Facial tics
- Insomnia
- Obsessive-compulsive disorder
- Phobias
- Post-traumatic stress disorder
- Psychosis
- Relationship problems (individual or couple's therapy)
- Schizophrenia

In most cases, it can be a very effective form of treatment without the use of medication, but in extreme cases, where the symptoms a patient is experiencing are severe, a doctor may suggest the use of medications to make it easier to get into a mental state where patients can effectively apply the strategies suggested as they go through the program.

How it Works on Anxiety and Depression

When dealing with anxiety disorders, one must first come to understand the true nature of anxiety. While unpleasant in many ways, a certain level of anxiety is necessary for life. Without it, we would find ourselves in an even worse predicament. Consider all the ways a healthy sense of anxiety can be of benefit.

Both anxiety and fear are natural forms of emotions. They serve as your body's personal alarm system and can occur as a warning sign that there may be some kind of risk or harm present. Fear, a heightened sense of anxiety, appears when a person is literally faced with a dangerous situation. Anxiety occurs when they "expect" that something unpleasant is about to happen.

A good example of this is taking a ride on a roller coaster. The feeling you get as the car is slowly pulled up that first big hill. You are in anticipation of what you know is about to happen as soon as you reach the top. Fear is the feeling you get when you are plummeting down the hill.

Both emotions are warnings and can trigger all sorts of bodily sensations. They tap into our flight-or-fight response so that we can quickly respond to those warnings, allowing us to flee, freeze, or fight. These instinctive emotions have been a part of us for as long as the human race has existed. It is a highly developed system that allows us to react quickly without having to put forth a lot of effort. They make it possible for us to have an automatic response.

The problem with these emotions is evident when they become overactive. It is natural for humans to have a very active imagination that allows our minds to create certain scenarios that we may encounter. For example, you may be anticipating how a certain job interview will play out. Your mind may conjure up something good or something very bad, both could result in anxiety even though there is no assurance that what you imagined will actually happen. This is evidence that our internal alarm system can be triggered even when there is no real threat to deal with.

The natural progression is that if our automatic thoughts are negative, we will respond accordingly. As a result, if we have conjured up images of a bad interview, our reactions could be so strong that we can take some very negative actions that could harm us in some way. For example, we might refuse to show up for the interview, we might choose to apply for a job that we find less challenging or risky, or we might become so flustered that we blow the interview altogether causing our worst fears to come true. These choices could actually have a very negative effect on our lives causing us even more harm in the future.

Anxiety and depressive disorders can appear in a variety of forms. Episodes may be occasional or they may be constant. If these automatic thoughts are not addressed, they will only become more sensitive starting a spiral effect that will send a person deeper and deeper into a level of anxiety that will be even more difficult to get out of.

CBT is most effective because it works to correct those automatic thoughts. Those spontaneous thoughts we all have that spring to mind without prompting. Automatic thoughts start before we are born and will continue unabated until we take our last breath. It is our brain's way of processing the millions of bits of information it is constantly receiving from our five senses: sight, sound, smell, taste, and touch. If the brain receives any input from these sources under a stressful situation, it can create unfounded assumptions about a given situation or possible outcome. These negative assumptions create an unhealthy internal dialog that could build up to a point that it prevents an individual from progressing when faced with similar circumstances. Unless this internal dialog is corrected, the resulting negative emotions or behavior could take control causing the person to be paralyzed to the point of inaction or to exercise complete avoidance.

So, how can you tell if you have normal anxiety or have a disorder? Mental health professionals often refer to the *Diagnostic and Statistical Manual of Mental Disorders (DSM-5)* for the guidelines for making a diagnosis. An anxiety disorder is diagnosed when:

- The anxiety one experiences are excessive: being afraid of snakes may be normal but being petrified of worms would be considered extreme.
- The anxiety is constant and can last for weeks or months at a time: there are different time frames for each type of disorder. For example, when panic disorder symptoms last for a month or more, it can be diagnosed as an anxiety disorder. However, for generalized anxiety disorder, the symptoms must be present for a minimum of six months.
- The anxiety itself causes more anxiety: when a person becomes really upset by the mere fact that they are experiencing anxiety.
- The anxiety interferes with a person's normal activities: when you can't walk outside of your home, go into a public place, or can't work on a job because of the heightened level of anxiety.

There are several different types of anxieties that could be considered an anxiety disorder. They are very different from each other, so before treatment can be started, one must understand exactly what type of disorder they have.

Phobias: Phobias are powerful and irrational fears of a particular object or situation. Common phobias could be a fear of anything from snakes to something that is part of the natural environment. Most common forms of phobias might be an extreme fear of storms, flying, elevators, spiders, and even people. In many cases, these start with a traumatic experience, but not always. Sometimes, the actual cause of a phobia is never discovered.

Social Anxiety Disorder (SAD): These are fears of social situations. In these types of cases, the fear is often confined to the fear of embarrassment. SAD is different from other phobias because it often involves the mind "guessing" about what is going to happen or what someone else might be thinking. With other phobias, we may know that the thing we're imagining can actually happen. We know about dog and snake bites; there is plenty evidence of the consequences of such events, but social phobias are more likely related to what one might be thinking rather than as a result of what they believe.

Panic Disorders: Panic disorders usually come about without warning. Many often mistake a panic attack for a disorder, but panic attacks that might be experienced are usually the symptom of the fear or phobia of a certain situation.

The attacks come on suddenly like a loud alarm going off in the body. The sympathetic nervous system instantly triggers a "fight-or-flight" response that is very physical. It releases a huge dose of adrenaline into the system to help prepare the body for danger. As a result, the person will experience:

- Rapid heartbeat
- Faster and deeper breathing
- Dizziness
- Profuse sweating
- Digestive problems
- Tense muscles

A person may experience some of these symptoms or all, but the concept here is that the symptoms are not just a little change but are quite extreme.

Agoraphobia: Interestingly enough, agoraphobia is not a very specific phobia but is the fear of being in places where you feel it would be bad to have a panic attack. This causes the person to avoid public areas such as movie theaters, shopping centers, public transportation, etc. If they go anywhere at all, it is usually in the company of another person they feel is safe and would be able to help them if something were to happen. In extreme cases, the patient is reluctant to leave the house at all and may squirrel away inside for years at a time.

General Anxiety Disorder (GAD): This disorder presents itself as a persistent and pervasive sense of worry. It is not the normal concerns of everyday life that most people have but is so intrusive that it interrupts sleep, keeps the individual from concentrating which leaves them to feel exhausted all the time. Unlike other anxiety disorders, GAD is also evidenced by anxiety and worries that are spread out over a number of different areas. It is not specific to a single type of fear, thus the name of General Anxiety Disorder. The individual's life is plagued by a never-ending worry about "what ifs" to the point that they can no longer function normally.

People who suffer from panic attacks, phobias, obsessive thoughts, and a never-ending stream of worries about everything will gain the most from CBT. This type of therapy, unlike medications, treats much more than just the symptoms that you may have. It can help to reveal the underlying causes of those incessant worries and fears. As a result, patients learn to relax and see each situation in a completely fresh and less intimidating way. They become better at coping and learn how to think through all of their problems.

There are many different types of anxiety disorders, so each session will be tailored to the specific problem of each patient. For example, for those who may be struggling with obsessive-compulsive disorder (OCD), their treatment will differ greatly from someone who is struggling with an anxiety attack.

The therapist will work with them to first identify the negative thought and then teach them through guided sessions on how to challenge those thoughts. For example:

Negative thought:	What if I have a panic attack on the subway? I'll pass out!
Distortion:	Believing that only the worst can happen.
Challenge:	Have you ever passed out on the subway before? It's unlikely that you will pass out on the subway.
Negative thought:	If I pass out, terrible things will happen.
Distortion:	Expectations clearly out of proportion with reality.

Challenge:	If I do pass out, it'll only be for a few seconds. That's not so bad.
Negative thought:	People will think I'm crazy.
Distortion:	Drawing conclusions you know nothing about.
Challenge:	People are more likely to show concern and help.

In the beginning, these thought challenges will be guided with the therapist, but in time, the patient will learn to do these themselves. For milder cases, an individual can work these out for themselves with the use of a CBT workbook. Negative thinking doesn't just happen all on its own but is an accumulation of a lifetime of negative influences. While it sounds simple here, it can be quite difficult to remold one's thinking into something that is more positive. Those suffering from anxiety and depression disorders will:

- Learn to identify anxiety and how it feels in the body
- Learn skills to help them to cope and relax to counteract the anxiety
- Learn to confront their fears (real or not)

Of all the psychological disorders you can find, anxiety is by far the most common.

- 18% of anxiety disorders are phobias
- 13% are social anxiety disorders
- 9% are general anxiety disorders
- 7% are panic disorders
- 4% are agoraphobia

Depressive Disorders

Depressive disorders come in a different form. Many may start with some type of injury that renders them unable to function for a time. This triggers a train of losses or disappointments of many of the things the person may use to enjoy. The loss of these once fulfilling activities starts him on a downward spiral where he begins to believe that he doesn't deserve them or that he's done something that has triggered the loss.

A depressive disorder can make it difficult to function in any capacity. They may feel like everything they do is ten times harder than it used to be. It could feel like trying to pull themselves out of a quicksand and they may feel that they are so pathetic or worthless that it is not worth putting up the effort.

Most people only know depression as a feeling of sadness, but its symptoms can vary widely depending on the type of depression they are experiencing. It can present itself in many forms. In many cases, the patient has no idea that he or she is dealing with depression, because often, the symptoms do not present themselves as they would expect.

Major Depressive Disorder: Another term for someone who is "clinically depressed" is a major depressive disorder. This can be described as a person who feels low for the better part of the day. However, while this is a very common symptom, it is not necessary for them to feel an overwhelming sense of sadness to be considered depressed. It could be evident in their lack of interest in any activities, many of which they may have used to enjoy.

At the same time, they may sleep excessively, eat more than usual (whether they are hungry or not), or stop eating altogether. They feel exhausted and have a hard time concentrating on what they need to do or even making decisions.

While we all have a tendency to feel bad about ourselves at one time or another, those who are clinically depressed feel so bad about themselves that they believe they are completely worthless and are at a very high risk of suicidal tendencies, so they need to be watched carefully.

According to DSM-5, there are nine different symptoms of depression; five are needed to be observed in order to be diagnosed as clinically depressed. Because of this, the condition of depression may look very different from one person to the next.

Persistent Depressive Disorder: There are ebbs and flows of a major depressive disorder, where the individual may feel up and good at times but at other times, they may struggle to even get out of bed. With a persistent depressive disorder, however, the symptoms may seem to be more chronic. To be diagnosed with a persistent depressive disorder, they have to experience symptoms consistently for a minimum of two years before they are diagnosed. In addition, they need to display at least two more symptoms listed in the DSM-5.

With a PDD, the symptoms can be milder, but its negative effects can be extreme. While the symptoms may not appear to be as severe as an MDD, one can never assume that its effects are not as bad. At times, the symptoms can be even more destructive because of their chronic nature, as the individual never gets any sort of relief from the pervasive symptoms.

Premenstrual Dysphoric Disorder: This type of depression usually appears just before and for several days into a woman's menstrual period. It is important to understand that this is not the same thing as PMS (premenstrual syndrome). The condition is much more extreme with women displaying volatile mood swings and irritability. In addition to feeling anxiety, they can often show physical symptoms as well including breast tenderness and bloating. The symptoms should appear before or during most of her menstrual cycles for as much as a year before being accurately diagnosed.

Getting diagnosed with an anxiety or a mood disorder is not always easy. In fact, the process can be quite complex. Each form of depression has to have a number of different labels that identify exactly which type of depression the person may be dealing with and its nature. In addition to the main symptoms listed above, there may be seasonal depression, postpartum, a form of melancholy, single, and recurrent episodes. Whatever the case, there is a good chance that applying CBT techniques can help to manage all of these symptoms. One of the first things an individual needs to do is to get an official diagnosis. Once the diagnosis is completed, the next step is to sit down and work out how it is affecting you in order to determine the goals you want to work towards and a time frame in which to complete them in.

How CBT Helps With Substance Abuse

While CBT is most often used for anxiety and depressive disorders, there are many more mental health issues that it can also help with. It has been highly effective in preventing the relapse of problem drinking and drug addictions. These are common behavioral patterns that can be readjusted by redirecting the thought processes that trigger the abuse of many substances.

A key element of CBT is teaching the patient to anticipate situations and give them practical strategies to help them to cope effectively when these conditions arise. These strategies could include things like analyzing consequences before a decision is made to use the substance, self-monitoring themselves so they can identify cravings at the onset, and avoid situations where they might be at a higher risk of using.

By learning to develop strategies that will help them to better deal with cravings and those situations where they will find themselves more vulnerable, they can reduce and eventually eliminate their use of these substances

With the treatment for substance abuse, the objective of CBT is to:

- Help the individual to identify those situations where they are more likely to use alcohol or drugs
- Help them to develop strategies to avoid such situations
- And to identify common problems and triggers, which could cause them to abuse substances

This is done through two major components: function analysis and skills training.

With functional analysis, the therapist and the individual works to identify certain thoughts, feelings, and environments that historically have led to substance abuse. From this, they are able to determine the level of risk the patient is likely to face, or under what situations could expose them to a potential relapse.

CBT also will give them special insight into what started them on the path to substance abuse in the first place. Then they will give them coping strategies, so they are equipped to handle similar situations in the future.

With skills training, the individual will learn better coping skills. They will work on unlearning those old habits that took them in the wrong direction and replacing them with healthier habits that will be of benefit to them. In other words, they will be educated about how to change their thinking so that they are better able to deal with the varying situations that will trigger more episodes in the future.

To date, more than 24 different trials have been conducted with substance abusers of all sorts including those who are addicted to alcohol, cocaine, marijuana, opiates, and tobacco. In each of these studies, CBT has proven to be one of the most effective forms of treatment in helping to restructure their recovery. However, it is not the catchall answer for everyone. Because each person is different in the nature of their problems, everyone will respond to this type of treatment in a different way. Still, the results speak for themselves and if you or someone you care about is struggling with some form of substance abuse, there is a good chance that they will learn something and gain some benefit from incorporating CBT into their lives.

Chapter 2: How CBT Can Help With…

We live in unpredictable times and every one of us may be expected to address a number of issues at any given time. It can be a pretty stressful life for most of us. However, if someone is dealing with intrusive thoughts on top of the problems they face, it can become a complex maze that they may struggle desperately to get out of.

Dealing with any problem is not really the issue for these people. When a situation arises, the difficulty occurs with the manner in which he or she may address it. If their solution is based on distorted thinking, it can create a myriad of new problems in addition to creating a snowball effect. People who are plagued with unrealistic and intrusive thoughts are usually more reactionary rather than taking a proactive approach.

CBT's goal-oriented approach encourages a hands-on and more practical direction which teaches the patient that there is a means to an end. They do this by making a comparison between where the individual is at the start of the problem and then working out the best path to take to achieve the set goal. The ultimate goal is to change the thought pattern, which in turn, will change how they feel, and by extension, their behavior. In this way, CBT has been used to treat a wide variety of problems that range from sleep disorders to relationship issues.

On the surface, the logic of CBT is very simple: change one's negative thinking to positive thinking. However, this is not always easy. It requires that the person first learn to identify the negative thought processes they have. This requires them to take a hard look at themselves and give an honest appraisal of how they really think.

This may involve applying a little mindfulness and seeing their thoughts as a neutral person. When they see that their views are overly negative or overly positive. They will be compelled to learn to adopt a more balanced view of themselves, those around them, and their environment; viewing everything as a neutral person. This kind of adjustment takes time, as they may not fully realize just how far their thinking has strayed from the normal way of things.

Patients need to learn how to identify when their thoughts are triggering negative emotions and when to stop them before this happens. Then, they need to examine those thoughts honestly to determine if they are truly giving a fair and honest appraisal of the situation; how realistic they are and how damaging those thoughts are to them.

This helps them to avoid falling into thinking traps (negative ways of viewing things) so they don't fall into the problem situation in the first place. These mental traps could become major landmines that could quickly throw them into a world of trouble. These thinking traps are often negative words they would never say to others, but they say it to themselves.

Consider if you don't like people talking down to you, then why would you do the same thing to yourself? It is possible to hurt your own feelings and damage your self-esteem. One of the first traps they are taught to avoid is those that you do without realizing it. Through CBT, you learn to identify these habits, stop them, and then change that point of view.

Problem-Solving With Depression or Anxiety

Problem-solving therapy empowers people, so they are better equipped to change the circumstances of their lives. They learn to work through challenges and take a proactive approach to their problems. Through this type of program, patients learn how to manage these issues through several core components:

Addressing the Problem: There are many approaches that people can take when they deal with a problem. Some will naturally be more submissive in the decision-making phase, others will apply avoidance techniques, and others will be more aggressive. Whatever strategy one takes, the treatment will focus on the developing thoughts and attitudes one applies to solve their particular problems. It will work to identify certain weaknesses and address those with cognitive steps and techniques.

Defining the Problem: The next step is to define exactly what the problem is so they have a clear understanding of what they are dealing with. For example, a client may see that they are constantly under stress while at work. The first conclusion might be that they are dealing with anxiety. However, other factors may be at the root of the anxiety. They may not be assertive enough on the job and as a result, are allowing people to overburden them with additional work. They may not be setting boundaries, so people do not know their limits, and this is adding to their stress level.

Developing Strategies to Help Them Cope: Together, they work with the therapist to outline very specific steps that will help them to change their behavior and provide a number of possible solutions to the problem. By taking into consideration a wide variety of possibilities that will work, they may feel more empowered and actually begin to believe that they can work it out.

Execution: Finally, when they have broken down their goals into smaller easy-to-achieve steps, they are better capable of taking the necessary action to solve the problem. As they progress through the different steps, they will gain confidence and are more likely to follow the plan and successfully solve their problems.

There have been many studies that have definitively shown that this type of therapy can be a very useful form of therapy on its own. However, it can be even more effective when it is included in a full CBT treatment plan, yielding even better results.

CBT with Sleep Disorders

Often, people who struggle with sleep disorders have an extremely difficult time dealing with life in general. With a lack of sleep, they will naturally suffer from low energy, and when their energy is low, they are likely to also have poor nutrition. Poor nutrition contributes to brain fogginess, and in the end, they are caught up in a vicious cycle that is difficult for them to break free from. CBT can help them to get to the root cause of their sleep disorder and correct the wayward thoughts that are interrupting their ability to sleep.

Insomnia, a common sleep disorder that affects many people, has been treated very effectively through CBT. The condition makes it hard to fall asleep and even more difficult to stay asleep once you do.

CBT-1, the form of therapy used for sleep disorders, is a structured program that helps you to replace those intrusive thoughts with the kind of habits that will be more conducive to getting good sleep. The right treatment used for your sleep disorder will depend on a variety of factors.

Stimulus Control Therapy: This form of therapy focuses on removing the factors that may be contributing to your inability to sleep. These could include setting up routines that will support a better bedtime routine, one that is more conducive to sleep. It may involve setting up a consistent time to go to bed and wake up, avoiding naps, and restricting the use of the bed for anything other than sleeping and sex. No eating, watching TV or talking on the phone while in bed.

Sleep Restriction: This treatment would prevent you from being in bed for too long a time without sleeping. If you're in bed for more than 20 minutes without sleeping, it can add to your sleep deprivation. With sleep restriction, the amount of time you spend in the bed is shortened to only when you can sleep. Once you have developed a healthy sleep period, this time can be extended until you reach a point where you can sleep through the night.

Sleep Hygiene: This will get rid of those negative habits that interrupt sleep. Smoking, too much caffeine late in the day, consuming too much alcohol, or lack of exercise can all be part of the problem. CBT therapy can help you to reduce or eliminate those habits so that you can more easily relax before bedtime.

Sleep Environment Improvement: This treatment focuses on habits that create a positive sleep environment. Strategies to keep the room dark, quiet, and at the right temperature can be very effective in teaching a patient to relax.

Passive Awakeness: This focuses on avoiding any attempt to fall asleep. Interestingly enough, worrying about not being able to sleep can contribute to one's inability to sleep. Learning how to not worry about it allows the body to relax so you can drift off to sleep more easily.

Biofeedback: Once a person is aware of how his biological functions are operating, they can learn how to manipulate them. Many of these factors can interrupt one's sleep. A person's heart rate, tension in their muscles, or body temperature can all interfere with their regular sleep patterns. Learning how to mentally adjust these and other biological elements can put your body into a more comfortable state where sleep will come easily.

Whether your sleep disorder is mild or extreme, using CBT-1 can help all sorts of problems. Even if the cause of the problem is physical, as in cases of chronic pain, or mental, as in cases of anxiety and depression, the problems tend to go away once the right kind of therapy is undertaken, all without negative side effects. It will require consistent practice and applications, but the longer you stick with it, the better the end results will be.

Chapter 3: Common Causes of Mood Disorders

When you first start Cognitive Behavioral Therapy, one of the first things you will have to do is to identify the root cause of your dysfunction. In nearly every case, the problem lies in your automatic thoughts. These are at the heart of the theory behind this type of treatment.

Automatic thoughts are known to pop into your mind without any effort. They are the brain's means of processing all of the information it is receiving from the environment. These thoughts do not represent any type of fact about the situation that it is processing, which is why they can cause so much damage. The type of automatic thoughts that appear immediately after dealing with a specific situation can be referred to as your "instinctive" response. They appear so quickly that there is literally no time to reason on the situation or apply logic, so relying on them to make decisions is often the reason why a person would display dysfunctional behavior.

In your first session with the therapist, you will learn to recognize your dysfunctional thoughts. Likely, you will backtrack from a specific experience in order to identify the actual thought that triggered your negative emotion. You should pay close attention to any thoughts that cause you to have a reflex change in mood in response to it. These are the dangerous thoughts that are connected to what you truly believe about something.

A good example of this may be how you react when you watch someone speaking in public. Your knee-jerk reaction to what is said is a reflection of what you truly believe about that situation. If there is a great deal of approval from the audience but you don't like it, your mind won't take the time to contemplate his words. If you are applying your feelings to yourself, your thoughts might reflect a general negativity about yourself. "People will never respond to me like that," or "I wish I was as happy as he is." These personal negative reflections are labeled as "dysfunctional automatic thoughts." These beliefs will trigger equally negative feelings that are, in turn, triggering certain behaviors you want to change.

To address these thoughts through CBT, you will first have to figure out if your negative thought patterns are caused by a physical imbalance in your system. There are several things that could tell if you are physically out of balance.

Chemical Imbalances

There is quite a bit of dispute about whether chemical imbalances are a real cause of mental disorders or not. It was once believed that chemical imbalances are the result of too much of some chemicals or too little being produced in the brain. These chemicals, called neurotransmitters, are used to aid in the communication between the neurons of the brain. You may have heard of many of them: dopamine, serotonin, and norepinephrine are just a few. It was generally understood in the world of psychiatry that mental disorders like depression and anxiety are usually the result of these chemicals being out of balance in the brain.

These types of disorders can be extremely complex, and finding a definitive answer to your problem is not always easy. However, a good way to assess whether or not you're dealing with these types of imbalances is by looking at the symptoms.

- Feeling sad, worthless, or empty
- Tendency to overeat
- Loss of appetite
- Inability to sleep
- Sleeping too much
- Feeling restless
- Irritable
- A constant feeling of dread
- Listless
- Not wanting to associate with others
- Lacking empathy
- Feeling numb all over
- Extreme mood swings
- Inability to concentrate
- Suicidal thoughts
- Thoughts of hurting others
- Inability to perform normal everyday activities

- Hearing voices that are not there
- Substance abuse

While we don't know the exact cause of these imbalances, many researchers believe that it could be a combination of genetics, our environment, and social influences on our lives. It is even unclear how these are able to affect us and create mental disorders. What we do know is that even if you do have a chemical imbalance, it is not the end of the situation. By applying the techniques of CBT, it is possible to change to more positive behaviors, which can, in time, correct them.

Dopamine: The brain uses dopamine to control both your movements and your emotional responses. When it is balanced properly, it is an essential component for physical and mental wellbeing. It also helps facilitate important brain functions like your mood, your ability to sleep, how you learn, concentration, motor control, and even the ability to remember things. If you are low in dopamine, you are likely to feel:

- Muscle cramps
- Tremors
- Aches and pains
- Stiffness in the muscles
- Have difficulty keep your balance
- Constipation
- Trouble eating or swallowing
- An unexplainable weight loss or weight gain
- Gastroesophageal reflux disease
- Trouble sleeping
- Low energy
- Poor concentration
- Excessive fatigue
- Unmotivated
- Extreme sadness or hopelessness

- Poor self-esteem
- Anxiety
- Suicidal thoughts
- Low libido
- A lack of self-awareness

A dopamine deficiency may be linked to a number of mental health disorders. It may not be the direct cause, but it can certainly contribute to the severity of the problem.

Serotonin: While your body mostly uses serotonin in the digestive system, it can have an effect on every part of your body including your emotions. It can also be found in the blood platelets and in various parts of the central nervous system. It is made from tryptophan, an amino acid found in common foods like nuts, cheese, and red meat. When you have a deficiency of serotonin, it can trigger anxiety or depressive mood disorders.

Because it can be found throughout the body, it can have a major impact on everything from your emotions to your motor skills. It is the body's natural way of keeping the mood stable. It also helps with eating, digesting foods, and allowing us to relax enough so we can sleep. When you have a good balance of serotonin, your body can:

- Fight off depression
- Control levels of anxiety
- Heal wounds better
- Maintain good bone health

You will also find that you are:

- Happier
- Emotionally stable
- Calmer
- Less anxious
- Able to concentrate better

If your serotonin levels are too high, it could be a sign of carcinoid syndrome, a condition that causes tumors in the small intestine, bronchial tubes, appendix, or the colon. Your doctor could determine your serotonin levels through a simple blood test. Symptoms of a serotonin deficiency are:

- Poor memory
- Signs of aggression
- Low or depressed mood
- Anxiety
- Cravings for sweet or starchy foods
- Insomnia
- Low self-esteem

You are equally at risk of major health problems if your serotonin levels are too high or too low, so it is very important to keep a good balance to protect not just your physical health but your mental health as well.

Other Imbalances: There are other chemicals in the brain that can have an effect on your moods and emotions. However, as we now understand how the brain works, it is important to realize that there is still an ongoing debate as to what extent these imbalances actually cause or affect the moods and emotions.

It should be a foregone conclusion that no person is born with these anxiety disorders. Whether the imbalances are a result of one's genetic make-up or are from the environment, it is clear that there is only one way that we know of to fix it. We have already learned that habits and behaviors are developed by using the neural pathways in the brain to send signals back and forth. Since these chemicals are responsible for facilitating that communication, it only stands to reason that the best way to treat imbalances is to strengthen those connections.

Because it focuses on those automatic thoughts, even if there is a chemical imbalance, it can be reversed by regular practice of the routine steps and strategies a patient will learn while working through the steps of CBT.

Chapter 4: Understanding Your Moods and the Way You Think

Understanding your mood and the way you think is not easy. As you analyze a particular situation where you have been feeling those negative emotions, you have to start with a serious self-analysis. Your goal is to figure out exactly what kind of thoughts and feelings you have lying just underneath the surface. You can do this by asking yourself some very pointed questions:

- What was I doing when I began to feel that way?
- Where was I?
- Is this the only place where I feel like this?
- What was my behavior like before and after this episode?
- What hidden beliefs do I have that are showing right now?
- What causes me to intensify those feelings?
- Who was I with?
- Am I the same with everyone or just certain people?

An honest answer to these types of questions can be very revealing. For example, a person may start to feel depressed when he is alone and away from other people. These types of questions help you to get to exactly why you have experienced those sudden mood changes. If you're a person that suddenly feels awkward and ashamed when you're in the gym, you may be harboring hidden beliefs in relation to your body image. If you start to feel negative emotions while out in public, it could mean that you have serious concerns about your abilities to perform in front of strangers.

After doing this type of exercise, most people are surprised when they learn so much about themselves this way. It can be alarming to discover that their automatic thoughts, which are often just fleeting in the mind, can have such power, triggering emotions unexpectedly as if they just came on without warning. Usually, these thoughts reveal a very specific issue and once you know what it is, you can now direct your energy to that particular thought process.

How to Diagnose Your Negative Thought Patterns

As you get started working your way through this stage of therapy, you must realize that no two people will have the exact same disorder. While they may have been diagnosed with the same label, your personal experience will be very different from someone else, because you bring to it your own personal body of experiences.

Even finding the answers to questions like the ones listed above are not easy to do. You may have to get a frank viewpoint from someone close to you and whom you can trust to get the ball rolling. Some complete the entire first session without learning what is at the heart of their problem. However, they will have learned how to start trying to think differently about their experiences.

This is not to be surprising. Most of us have gotten pretty good at hiding some of those negatives that permeate our lives every day and have done so for years. It's not likely that everything is going to come out in the first wash. Still, if you persist in this type of self-analysis, there is a very good chance that you will be able to identify many of the tricks and tactics you have created to cover up your true feelings about certain things.

As you go through this process, don't be afraid to look at every aspect of your life and not just in the obvious areas. It is quite often that the real trigger has little or no direct connection to where your thinking went awry. For example, you may be having a communication problem with your spouse. He or she may think you are distant, uncommunicative, or just has lost interest in the relationship. However, if you're dealing with a hidden anxiety or depression that started many years prior, it may still be affecting you and causing you to separate from your partner.

Imagine it this way. You are a child and you have a close and dear friend who died of a sudden illness. Your relationship was strong, and you were always very happy when with that person. However, their death suddenly left a huge void in your life. On the surface, you were able to eventually get over it and move on, but that pain was never clearly addressed. Now, in a relationship, you are afraid to commit that way to another person.

This kind of hidden pain could be what is causing those automatic thoughts that are firing in your brain.

- I can't commit to another person, they will leave me.
- I can't go through losing someone again in my life.
- It's not worth it. Everybody is going to die anyway.

A past loss may have been the real reason you don't trust or are afraid to communicate with your spouse. People die, friends move away, jobs are lost, and a myriad of other conditions could be behind the reason for your automatic thoughts. If you were a child when it happened, it is quite possible your grief was either not recognized or considered unimportant in a world where everyone else is in grief too. However, being able to learn the hidden secrets that are triggering those automatic thoughts can give you great insight on where they come from and why they are resurfacing. As a result, you have a basis for addressing the issue now and correcting those thoughts from a more realistic position.

Now, this may seem strange in light of what we said earlier; that a CBT therapist does not reach back into our past to find the root cause of a problem. This is true, however, as you begin to recognize these automatic thoughts, it is only a small step to making the connection between your past and the present.

Once you are able to identify those thoughts, there are several ways you can deal with them.

- If you feel the thought is indicative of a larger issue, you can choose to put all your energies into correcting that thought.
- If you feel that there is another problem that better identifies the issue, you can choose to focus on the two thoughts together.
- If you discover that there are other issues that are beginning to surface, you can put the initial thought aside and focus on the bigger and most important issues first.

After you have uncovered these hidden thoughts, the next step is to analyze each thought and rate them as to how important they are. If one thought seems to produce intense feelings in one way or another, it is likely the one that has the biggest impact.

Sometimes, it can be difficult to separate the different thoughts in your mind. In that case, it is helpful to keep a notepad nearby and write down the thoughts as they appear. As you write down each thought, make sure to also take note of what was happening when it occurred and the feelings it evoked. If you do this over a period of time (perhaps a week), you'll begin to notice a definite pattern emerge.

There are several different categories of automatic thoughts, and by journaling them as they happen, the patterns that emerge will help you to classify the type of thoughts you're having. Below is a list of some of the most common beliefs that many people develop that can trigger negative emotions.

- All or nothing: A person who believes everything is either black or white with no middle ground or gray area.
- Catastrophizing: A belief that every situation will produce the worst results.
- Discounting Positives: The belief that all positive experiences are false.
- Emotional Reasoning: Allowing one's negative feelings about a situation to be the deciding voice in their head.
- Jumping to Conclusions: Automatically concluding negative results for a situation with any evidence to back up assumptions.
- Labeling: The act of giving negative labels to ourselves or to other people. Calling yourself a loser or a failure rather than making the effort to change the quality you don't like.
- Magnification/Minimization: Putting a lot of emphasis on anything bad and downgrading anything good. Really stressing out about a mistake but not willing to accept compliments or acknowledge achievements.
- Negative Bias: Seeing only the bad in any situation and dwelling on the negative, despite the fact that there are many positives.
- Overgeneralizations: Using a single negative experience to represent every other similar event.

- Personalization: Believing that negative comments or actions from others are about you or believing that you are the cause of a bad event even when you had no connection with it.
- Should/Must statements: Having expectations based on what you believe should be done. These often stem from distorted perceptions of what others may believe about you and are likely not in the realm of reality. This could cause you to feel guilty for not meeting these abstract standards or often excessively high expectations.

Likely, as you read through this list, some of these dysfunctional automatic thoughts popped out at you. All of us have them from time to time, but if you think they are interfering with the progression in your life, then these should be the ones that you should focus your CBT exercises on.

Intrusive Thoughts

In our minds, we have many thoughts throughout the course of a single day. It is estimated that each of us has between 50-70,000 thoughts in a single 24-hour period. Most of them, we are able to quickly dismiss as insignificant and unimportant. But there are those disturbing thoughts that seem to get stuck in our brain and no matter what we do; we can't seem to get rid of them. They make us feel sad, frightened, and sometimes, even sick and can create a great deal of turmoil in our emotions.

The fact that they are so intrusive and they seem to camp out in our head can cause us even more distress; some to the point where they interfere with our regular routines and activities causing us to feel ashamed, guilty, or afraid. Anyone suffering from an anxiety disorder like OCD or PTSD can quickly relate to the kind of damage an intrusive thought like these can do.

These thoughts are always unpleasant and can even make you feel repulsed. They can include acts of violence, inappropriate sexual acts, or extreme criminal behavior. Those in relation to anxiety could be an excessive worry about future events or threats. Strategies learned through CBT can help to reduce their frequency and even help to lessen the extremes that they may take. Addressing these feelings would be a good way to start getting rid of them.

Examples of Some Intrusive Thoughts

- Unwanted sexual fantasies involving a child, animal, or another person close to you
- Unwanted sexual thoughts involving someone you work with but are not really attracted to.
- Imagining yourself committing a violent criminal act
- Fear that you will say the wrong thing in public
- Doubts about your religion or thoughts of doing something forbidden
- Doubts about your inability to do well on an exam you know you have prepared for
- Recurring thoughts about getting a rare disease
- Fear of death
- Repeated memories about something humiliating that happened in your childhood
- Repeated memories about a violent experience you had in the past

It is important to know at this point, that having intrusive thoughts is not indicative of a disorder. Everyone has them at one point or another. According to the *Journal of Obsessive-Compulsive Disorders,* 94% of people in the world have intrusive thoughts. It is one of the most common mental activities that we all have. What is different in those who have anxiety or depressive disorders is our reaction to those thoughts.

When you are healthy and your mental state is balanced, you are able to dismiss those thoughts and they won't upset you. When you struggle with those thoughts, it is because you have already associated a great deal of importance to them, which is an indication that you have an internal belief that they are true and accurate. In such cases, your mind starts to create a full narrative about those thoughts and conjure up its own implications about what kind of behavior you should display or what your future actions should be.

To counteract these thoughts, one of the first things you need to do is analyze them, so you can convince yourself that they are NOT true. This is especially important when you are dealing with some of the above thoughts that may be violent or otherwise inappropriate. It does not mean that you really want to do those things. If you continue to accept these things as true, then it can saddle you with an immeasurable sense of guilt and shame, which could cause you even more problems.

If you're struggling with these types of intrusive thoughts, then take some of the following steps to apply some CBT-based strategies to combat them.

Identifying Your Triggers for Anxiety and Stress

It is one thing to know what your problem is and another thing entirely to identify what is triggering the symptoms you're experiencing. Finding these triggers can be quite complicated as it is most likely due to a combination of factors including environmental, physical, and genetics. Even so, there are some events or personal experiences that may trigger certain forms of anxiety or, at the very least, make them much worse.

So, whether you're dealing with symptoms of anxiety, depression, or stress as a result of a genetic factor that you have no control over, the condition can actually deepen as a result of certain events or experiences you are having in your day-to-day life. These events, emotions, and experiences are called triggers.

These triggers can vary from one person to the next. However, in most cases, you're likely responding to several triggers at one time. It may seem, on the surface, that your reaction to a given situation comes completely out of nowhere, but in most cases, there is always something there, just underneath the surface. So, while it may be uncomfortable to do, it is important to root out your personal triggers, so you can take proactive steps in managing them. Below are some of the most common triggers that many people have.

Health Issues: Often, your own health may be playing a part in increasing your anxiety or depression. Diseases such as cancer or another type of chronic illness can trigger anxiety or even make it worse. Just getting a diagnosis of a disease like cancer can immediately evoke powerfully negative emotions that can be very difficult to combat.

To counteract this kind of trigger, you need to take a proactive approach by working together with your doctor and even discussing it with a therapist as they can give you strategies to help you manage your emotions as you go through your treatment.

Medications: The intrusive thoughts and negative emotions may be the result of the medication you're taking. While there is always a risk with certain prescription drugs of generating negative thoughts, even over-the-counter medications have been known to trigger anxiety and/or depression. This is due to the active ingredients that are working on your system. If you are able to dismiss these thoughts as a result of the medication, then great, but many people do not realize that the feelings they generate can trigger a number of side effects that could increase your level of anxiety.

Common medications that have been known to trigger anxiety/depression:

- birth control pills
- cold/flu medications to treat a cough and congestion
- weight loss medications

While for most people the symptoms will be non-existent or minimal, for those who have anxiety and depression disorders, these could pose a real problem. If after taking any medication, you find the intrusive thoughts are increasing or are causing negative emotions, speak with your doctor and get him/her to help you find an acceptable alternative.

Caffeine: Believe it or not, many people are addicted to caffeine, not realizing that it can be a very strong trigger for anxiety. Research has shown that people who are already susceptible to panic disorders or social anxiety disorders will be even more sensitive to the negative effects of caffeine.

To combat this, one of the best things you can do is to reduce or eliminate the amount of caffeine you consume and substitute it with other options for the stimulation you need.

Your Diet: Believe it or not, your diet can be a major contributing factor to your mental stability. Skipping meals, especially, can have a negative impact on your mental state. When you miss a meal, it causes your blood sugar levels to drop, which can trigger anxiety along with a host of other symptoms including that jittery feeling, nervousness, or agitation.

The best way to counteract this problem is to eat regularly and make sure that you have a diet that is balanced so that you get an adequate amount of nutrients in your system. The old rule that you must eat 3-5 meals a day is no longer encouraged. However, you need to make sure that your diet consists of enough nutrients to sustain you on a daily basis to prevent a drop in blood sugar.

Negativity: Nothing happens in our body unless it first happens in our mind, including anxiety. Your brain is the control center for your entire body so when you have anxiety, your self-talk can have a major impact on how you function. If you tend to be negative in your conversation or you are known for using a lot of negativity in reference to yourself, it can create a perpetual negative outlook on everything you do. Learn to use more positive expressions in your conversation and your feelings will soon follow. If you find this difficult, consider working with a therapist for a while until you learn to change your automatic conversation to a more positive and up-building form of self-talk.

Financial Problems: Debt can be a painful burden to undergo. Constant worry about not having enough or finding ways to save money can trigger a great deal of anxiety. While you may not be able to change your circumstances immediately, learning to manage these types of triggers can help to ease a lot of your intrusive thoughts. Working with a therapist can help guide you to a process that could help to get your mind to relax more.

Public Situations: Often, public events that include a lot of strangers can make one feel uncomfortable. The pressure of having to interact feels like walking through unfamiliar territory and can trigger many anxious feelings.

Worries about such occasions can be reduced by asking a trusted friend to accompany you so you won't feel like you're on your own. If your anxiety about these things is particularly intense, consider learning some coping mechanisms from a professional therapist so you are better equipped to managing them.

Conflict: Conflict in any form can be very stressful. Whether it is a relationship problem or a disagreement at work, these can trigger some of the worse anxiety you can deal with. If this is becoming a particularly stressful area for you, consider learning some conflict resolution strategies to learn better ways to control your feelings when conflicts arise.

Stress: We all face stress on a daily basis, but some of us get a bigger dose of it than others. Daily stress, when it is intense and constant, can trigger extreme anxiety symptoms along with other health problems. When under stress, you are likely picking up other habits that will contribute to your anxiety levels. Habits like over drinking, skipping meals, or insomnia will only intensify the anxiety.

Learning to first identify these habits and a few coping mechanisms will help you to handle them better so that they aren't allowed to overwhelm you.

Public Events/Performances: Situations that require you to speak or perform in public can be extremely stressful. Whether it is speaking up at a business meeting or competing at a special event, the stress can trigger all sorts of negative emotions and behaviors.

Try working along with a trusted friend or relative with some positive reinforcement to help you prepare and feel more comfortable beforehand. Regular practice with people you trust and even having them along with you for support can help you to feel more confident and relaxed.

Your Own Personal Triggers: It may be that you have triggers that are unique to you. These may not be so easy to identify. They could be something as simple as a smell that triggers something in your mind, the sounds of a song, the resemblance of a place or any number of things that can bring back a memory of a past traumatic event. This is common with people who suffer from PTSD. The triggers could be any number of things in their environment.

If you can identify these triggers, you can then take the next step to address them. Since these personal triggers are not likely to be those experienced by others, you will have to do a little bit of soul searching to uncover them. To help you find them, try these tips:

- Start keeping a journal where you take note of when your anxiety or depression is heightened. Record your thoughts and your feelings that occur at the same time. For example, answer the 5 W's (who, what, when, where, and why). After a while, you'll be able to see a certain pattern begin to emerge that will give you clues to your triggers.

- Be honest with yourself. Negative self-talk stems from a poor assessment of your true values and qualities. As long as you stay within that negative mode, it will be difficult to uncover the triggers to your anxiety and depression. Don't just accept the first thing that comes in your head. Be patient and be willing to look a little deeper into your life (past and present) to identify how they are making you feel.

- If the above two tips don't work, consider spending some time with a therapist. Even with all the effort you put out, some triggers have been so well-hidden that no matter what you do, it will be hard to pull out. Working with a professional can make it easier and take a lot of the pressure off of you.

Once you know and have identified your triggers, you have accomplished the first step in Cognitive Behavioral Therapy. Now, you can make a list of the problems you're facing and choose the ones you'd like to address and you're ready to move on to the next step in CBT.

Chapter 5: How it Treats Mood Disorders

During your first week of CBT, after you've identified the major problems you want to address, you'll have to go into setting goals for yourself. You know the type of anxiety and depression you're experiencing. Now, you need to work on a system for addressing these issues.

Practical Applications of CBT

Since no two forms of anxiety or depressive disorders are the same, there is no single way to deal with the challenges that each individual may face. Even those with the same diagnosis will have a different approach to their treatment. This means that before setting your goals, you need to have a pretty clear idea of what your specific problem is and what challenges you are facing. Once your unique situation is understood, then you can determine what kinds of changes are needed.

Generally, this is done at the first meeting with the therapist. You will be asked a number of questions that, at first, may not seem too important. For example, the therapist is likely to ask, *"Why are you here?"* Or in the case of trying CBT through the pages of this book, ask yourself, *"Why are you reading this book?"* This will prompt you to do an internal examination of your motivation for wanting to try CBT.

You might also spend some time determining what your strengths are. While you are looking at CBT to solve many of your problems, you will use your strengths as a tool to combat your struggles. There are several ways you can uncover your strengths. These are usually the things that people tend to recognize and admire about you, those qualities that others appreciate about you. Maybe, at this point, you don't see these qualities in yourself, but others do, so consider talking to someone close to you to find out just what they see in you that can be useful.

Next, you will need to take a step back and examine how your life is going at the moment. But don't just do a surface look at the conditions. Take extra notice of how the anxiety/depression is affecting you. There are several different aspects that you can examine closely.

- **Relationships:** Relationships often affect our overall health probably more than anything else. When your marriage is on the skids, it usually means that you're not satisfied with your life in general and that attitude can lead to some very negative thoughts. However, if you have a life full of positive relationships and full of supportive people, your outlook on life will have a more positive spin.

  As you examine the relationships, look at how your anxiety/depression is affecting them. For example, you may have a supportive relationship, but is your depression causing you to pull away and not spend as much time with them. Your anxiety may be causing you to live your life on a short fuse, constantly snapping at them or keeping you angry and on edge all the time.

  Don't just look at a relationship with your spouse or significant other but consider how it is playing out with your parents, siblings, friends, children, and even coworkers. Determine what is good in your relationships and what is not. How do you feel about the people who have moved out of your life (either by moving away, a death, or an unresolved disagreement)?

  Finally, think about your relationships that are affecting your anxiety/depression. Are they making you more anxious or more depressed? Take note of the answer to these questions because you will have to face them later.

- **Physical Health:** Next, take some time to analyze your overall health. Here, you want to consider your eating habits, the amount of physical activity you're involved in, and what substances you regularly use (alcohol, drugs, etc.) The goal here is to draw a line between your regular habits and how they are affecting you physically. These can easily affect your moods and cause anxiety or depression.

  As you consider health, think about any chronic health issues you're dealing with. Conditions like high blood pressure, diabetes, asthma, or other ongoing physical challenges can create huge inroads on your mood. If you're getting more physical exercise, how are you feeling about it? Do you enjoy your regular routine or do you find it a chore; something that you just have to get done? Is there a kind of activity that you enjoy more than others or do you just not like moving at all?

Look at how much alcohol or drugs you use each day. These include prescription drugs as well as less favorable ones. If you've had a problem with substance abuse in the past, this is something that you need to give some serious thought to.

The same weight should be given to your diet. If you are a stress eater, you are likely eating foods that are hampering your ability to function. You may not even realize that you're eating these foods. Another concern should be if you're eating enough or overeating. These habits will affect your weight, which could have a direct impact on your own self-image, self-esteem, and self-respect; all of which will affect your moods.

Sleep also can affect your physical health. If you're not getting enough or you're getting too much, it can have an impact on your daily routine. It can keep you from getting the kind of movement you need and even the kind of foods you eat. Look at any external factors that could be affecting your normal sleep routine: pets, partners, work, kids, etc.

All of us need to have some downtime. If we allow our lives to encroach on that time, our activity level will suffer. There are probably many things you'd like to be doing and many things you'd rather not be doing. If your activity level is too high, chances are that you haven't had much time to relax and destress. You may also not have had any time to do the kind of things you enjoy doing like sports, hobbies, travels, etc. You can be highly active and still not have time to do the things you enjoy.

You will take this week to examine your entire life to see how these factors and others are affecting your mood. Afterward, go back over everything you've noted and see how it affects you. First, look at how it has affected your life and your mood in the past, but then take some time to meditate on them. Note what negative emotions come out as you're doing this review. Common feelings that emerge just talking about these things include anxiety, joy, sorry, overwhelm, sad, melancholy, etc.

Setting Goals

With a better understanding of the problems you're coping with, it'll be much easier to set specific goals for you to start working towards. In CBT, goals need to be very specific, something that is measurable and within reach. You need to concentrate on the type of changes that will actually be meaningful to your life and that you feel you can reasonably achieve within a short amount of time.

It is important to not be vague at this point. Remember that CBT has a time limit. Whether the program you are on is six weeks or ten, your goals should reflect where you reasonably expect to be at that point. So, goals like "I want to be happier" or "I want to stop worrying so much," are not specific enough to maintain your motivation for the duration of the program.

Instead, your goals should have very defined parameters. "I want to be able to get up on time every day," or "I want to find time to do something I enjoy." Your goals need to relate directly to the specific problems you are facing. "I want to voice my opinion more in employee meetings."

You want to avoid making grand goals that will require a major commitment; instead, focus on something that is well within your ability to achieve in a one, two, or three-week period. When you make large goals that are far out of your scope of ability, try to set a series of smaller goals that will help you to reach the larger ones at a later date. You can have these larger expectations set for years later, but it's best to break them up into smaller steps with each one taking you closer and closer to what you ultimately want to achieve. As you progress through the program, you will develop a more balanced view of yourself, which will help you to improve in your ability to accomplish more.

Building Self-Esteem

When you are suffering from low self-esteem, CBT can be very practical in helping you to identify the source of your negative thoughts, and how it influences your behavior. By incorporating these strategies, those dealing with self-esteem issues can work their way towards a healthier lifestyle.

Because CBT works on your personal perception of yourself, the techniques learned will help you understand how your mind works to create its own meanings in your experiences, and then teach you how to reframe your negative views and alter them by focusing on building a more positive structure of thoughts to rely on.

Throughout your sessions, you may learn techniques like:

- **Cognitive Restructuring:** where you focus on thought patterns and their sources. By regular reflection on these patterns, you will learn how to analyze your method of judgment and start reshaping your perception into more realistic possibilities.

- **Behavioral Activation:** where you identify those situations that cause you discomfort or make you afraid. By engaging in this technique, you are encouraged to step out of your comfort zone and gradually learn how to insert yourself into new situations.

- **Assertiveness Training:** through assertiveness training, you learn to reclaim your self-confidence. Through this, you are motivated to step out of your area of comfort and assert yourself in various areas where you can build up your self-confidence.

- **Social Skills Training:** through this form of therapy, you learn to work on improving social skills. It may include learning how you interpret and analyze many of the social situations you may have to interact with. Since low self-esteem comes from a negative perception of interactions with others, learning how to interact in a variety of social environments will make you aware of how your mind processes these situations and redirects them into a more positive direction.

Anyone suffering from a low self-esteem can learn how their thoughts relate to their actions and how to reflect on their impact and work to redirect them in a healthier and more positive lifestyle.

Verbal Self-Talk

We talk to ourselves all the time, but when you have negative self-talk, it can be very damaging. We often say things to ourselves that we would never dare say to anyone else. Our stress does not just come from external input, but our own emotional makeup can significantly add to it. In fact, studies have shown that our emotional makeup can actually cause so much stress in our bodies that it changes our physical make-up. Negative self-talk can cause changes in a number of health issues including:

- Diarrhea/constipation
- Muscle tension and pain
- Ulcers
- Headaches
- Insomnia
- Teeth grinding
- High blood pressure
- Cold hands/feet

All of these, in addition to our anxiety and depression, we may be suffering from. Chronic stress depletes the body of the essential chemicals that it needs to function properly. When we lack these essentials, we leave ourselves open for a number of illnesses. However, it is possible for us to change the way we respond to external and internal elements and develop a more healing environment that will give us better health.

It starts with changing how we talk to ourselves. CBT can teach you how to control your negative reactions to different things by teaching you different ways to interpret your personal experiences. So, rather than berating yourself for a simple mistake, you could remind yourself of all the times you did things well.

This helps to reduce feelings of guilt, shame, and anxiety that are eroding our mental and physical health. By changing these negative thought patterns into positive affirmations, you will find your mental state will gradually begin to turn into another direction.

Counter Negative and Angry Feelings

Anger is a unique negative feeling. Unlike other negative emotions like sadness, guilt, or disgust, anger can also have a positive side to it, so all anger is not bad. Sometimes referred to as the moral emotion, it often appears in cases where morals are brought into question. Values like justice, fairness, and respect are at its core.

There may be times, however, when you may not be able to make the connection between the root of your anger and its actual cause. You may, for example, feel you are angry at one person or another, but the cause may be from an entirely different source. This makes anger a sort of an enigma. We know that it usually precedes aggression, so it pays to address this issue as soon as possible. Negative anger can be treated with several different approaches to CBT. In fact, studies show that in as little as 8-12 weeks, there have been some very promising results. Techniques such as problem-solving, relaxation strategies, and enhanced communication skills have all been very effective in helping people to handle their anger better.

Dealing With Feelings of Guilt

Everyone has to deal with guilt at some point. No matter who we are, holding onto the wrongs we've done in the past is probably the most common reason why people don't move forward. Most of it comes from having to deal with the consequences of the poor decisions we've made, but the feeling that one act can stop us from moving on with our lives can be crippling.

No matter what has been done in the past, since it is not possible to do those things over in a different way, when negative results occur, the guilt that results can become like a life sentence that you impose upon yourself. Getting rid of that guilt on your own can sometimes feel impossible.

Through CBT, you can be guided through looking at that past event and learn how to see it through fresh eyes; eyes that can see the situation from different angles. One particular technique applied is a technique called The Blame Pie. This tool helps you to see just how much control you had over the negative situation and that, in most cases, you were not totally responsible. It looks at each individual involved in the incident and divides the blame according to their contribution to the event. As each person is assigned a percentage of the blame, it literally lifts much of the weight off your shoulders.

This type of treatment, over time, can help someone to get past the weight of the responsibility they had and finally find themselves worthy of moving on to a better life.

Counteract Hopelessness

Sometimes, depression can become so deep that a person feels completely hopeless. Because depression is the result of negative thinking, recovery from something as severe as hopelessness can be painfully slow. Even if you have positive thoughts on occasion, when you reach the point of hopelessness, you may not allow them to surface long enough to reap the effects.

Normally, in a depressed state of mind, positive emotions are often squelched with more powerful, negative thoughts like "I don't deserve to be happy," or "I know this won't last." In their minds, even when they feel good, they are unable to enjoy it because they are waiting for the ax to fall.

Through CBT, identifying the pattern of thoughts that lead to negative behavior can be changed. Once you're better able to identify these patterns, you can recognize them when they arise, freeing your mind for more positive thoughts. This can be done in several phases:

- Identifying the problem and mapping out solutions.
- Write down more positive statements that can counteract the negative thoughts.
- Actively search for new opportunities to apply positive thoughts.
- Learn to accept disappointment as a normal part of life.

Chapter 6: Steps to Dealing with Mood Disorders and Depression

Preventing mood disorders and depression is at the heart of Cognitive Behavioral Therapy. It has a multilevel approach that starts small and builds, helping patients to change their thought processes in everything they do. With each step, they celebrate small advances that will help them to gradually get closer and closer to their goals.

The first phase of the therapy involves identifying the problem they are facing, which is generally the result of automatic and intrusive thoughts. This is a crucial phase of the therapy as it defines a starting point for the treatment needed. Without a solid knowledge of the problem, it would be difficult to target the right strategies and techniques to deal with it directly.

The second phase is a period of goal setting where they can work on where they want to be within a set timeframe. After identifying the biggest issues you may be facing, it is much easier to map out a series of steps that will help you to focus on the changes you want to make.

In phase three, you will need to identify the challenges and obstacles you will be facing that will likely get in the way of your goals. No path will be easy as you will have to deal with a variety of setbacks along the way. You can decide to use them as a roadblock preventing your progress, as an obstacle that will require you to make a detour on your path to success, or as a stepping stone used to help you to get to where you really want to be.

Phase four deals with learning how to challenge your automatic and intrusive thoughts. In this phase, patients learn how to separate reality from the exaggerated thoughts they normally have. Once these negative thoughts have been identified, they can be challenged by a series of questions that forces them to use logic to come to a more reasonable conclusion. At this point, you will need to look for factual evidence that will contradict your embedded beliefs. Once those beliefs have been identified and successfully refuted, then you can learn how to use the evidence to refute those beliefs. Over time, those beliefs will diminish and be replaced by more realistic ones.

Phase five helps with identifying even more automatic assumptions and beliefs.

Now that the automatic thoughts have been identified, this phase takes it another step forward and isolates the deeper core beliefs that all people have. These are the ones that are more absolute and less flexible. They most likely have been formed in childhood, and unless changed, will stay with you throughout your life, getting reinforced over the years with each experience you have.

This phase is the best stage to address these issues because many of us are reluctant to accept that these thoughts are wrong until they have addressed their own automatic thoughts first. Challenging these beliefs is often like challenging who you are as a person because they have been deeply embedded in your mind for years to come.

Phase Six focuses on changing the behavior. Up until this point, all of the exercises are dealing with the cognitive activity in the mind. These changes can now begin to extend outward involving participation in different activities and events giving special attention to those that will deliver a more positive mood.

For those dealing with depression, participating in these activities is crucial to lifting the mood. In this phase, the focus should rely heavily on avoidance issues, depression, anxiety, and phobias. Its goal is to boost self-confidence so you are more comfortable engaging in more meaningful activities.

Phase Seven deals with the problem-solving strategies you will need. It brings home the main point of Cognitive Behavioral Therapy; convincing your mind that everything is all right and that any problems that come up, you are capable of handling. While challenging your negative thoughts and beliefs will produce good results, the ability to master the skills taught in the problem-solving phase will be the most effective in helping to ease behavioral issues.

It is important to note that each of these seven steps can help you to move closer to your goal, it will not work well for everyone. Those who are suffering from severe depression, emotional trauma, and those mental illnesses that are considered to be extreme won't likely be enough. Most of the exercises and strategies you learn in CBT can be done and practiced on your own, but if you're dealing with extreme emotional instability, then you may need more guided therapy to help you get back on the right path.

The problem-solving phase involves several steps:

1. Identify the problem and the specific elements you need to address.

2. Brainstorm possible solutions.
3. Evaluate each solution to determine the pros and cons of each.
4. Choose an optimal solution and then choose a backup.
5. Create a plan of action.
6. Execute the plan.
7. Review results and make needed adjustments.
8. If the problem is not resolved, start again at step 1.

At this phase, you will also need to review your lifestyle habits. Modifications will likely be necessary as an aid to improve how your brain processes thoughts. You will be coached in matters of sleep, eating, physical activity, and meditation.

Most people will see impressive results after applying these methods over a period of several weeks. The most common approach is to take one or two weeks to address each step. After you have successfully met the challenges of one phase, then do not hesitate to move on to the next one. Hesitation could interrupt the momentum you've developed and could cause you to lose your steam.

Chapter 7: Multimodal Model

As you can see, there are multiple ways that CBT can help a person to counteract their negative tendencies. With their Multimodal strategy, the technique gets a little more in-depth with a closer look at the seven different aspects of the human personality.

With this model, therapy consists of using a variety of models at one time, all of which are able to be adapted to many situations because they are completely interactive. They also share the same core beliefs that an individual will use to build his thought processes on. They consist of a combination of several elements including:

- Their Biological and genetic makeup
- The Effects of their experiences
- The Sensations that exist between thoughts, feelings, and behavior
- The Imagery that occurs in their own minds, mental images both negative or positive
- Their Cognition, or the way they think whether positive or negative
- Their Interpersonal relationships with others
- Their Drugs/biology, or their physical experiences, or the use of substances

These are considered the core of this type of therapy. They can be easily identified with the acronym BASIC ID. Each of these modalities is used to help narrow down the areas in which the coaching sessions should focus on.

The beauty of the Multimodal Model is that it recognizes that different people will respond to different modalities. You may be capable of handling your problems on your own while others will rely heavily on the support of others, and others may prefer to deal with their problems through certain activities. All of these can be incorporated into the seven areas of the BASIC ID, so it is possible to focus on those strategies that will allow them to overcome the problems they face in a manner that they can feel more comfortable with.

The goal of MMD is to help the individual make the necessary changes so they can make the transition from their current state of mind to a more progressive and adaptable mental state. MMD is often used in highly complex cases of depression and performance anxiety. Those who benefit the most are experiencing negative behavior so extreme that their lives are paralyzed to the point that they are unable to move forward. Their careers and their families are already at risk or on the verge of falling apart. Some have a level of fear that has reached a climax that it has had a heavy impact on nearly all seven of the modalities, and an intervention is likely the only possible solution.

Its success can be attributed to the principle that by approaching several issues at the same time, an individual may find themselves dependent on substances or other crutches to deal with them. It could be a combination of health problems, emotional issues, and financial distress all at the same time. Each case severe enough to be addressed on their own but through MMD, it is possible to address all of these issues at the same time to facilitate a speedier recovery.

The Seven Modalities You Should Know About

Because most psychological problems tend to be multifaceted, it is necessary to start by understanding each of the seven modalities that are actually affecting you. When you consider that many of the intervention techniques that people naturally turn to are substances, it is helpful to give even more consideration to the last modality, drugs or substances, as they will hold many techniques that can reveal your inner self. Now, let's take a closer look at each one of them to see how they are used in CBT.

Behavior: This aspect of MMD takes a close look at everything a patient does. This includes his habits, gestures, actions, etc. Some of his behaviors will be healthy while others will not be. Unhealthy behaviors that require particular attention could be those that are destructive, immoral, childish, illegal, impulsive, controlling, or otherwise, inappropriate.

Most patients will seek therapy because their unwanted behaviors are causing problems in their lives. Practices such as overeating, excessive drinking, hoarding, rebellion, self-mutilation, etc. are the most common. The goal is to change the behavior itself through techniques like modeling, desensitization, and aversive conditioning. The trick is that nearly all unwanted behaviors are connected to the other modalities as well, so by including this in the MMD therapy sessions, there is a much higher chance of success and the prevention of a relapse.

Affect: This modality refers to the inner feelings and emotions you are experiencing. Throughout the process, you may feel a wide range of emotions, but the focus of the therapy is to address the feelings you don't like. So, while you may feel happy, sad, afraid, frustrated, and bored, the sessions will likely involve the negative emotions first. Many who are seeking therapy for other reasons will often find that these emotions are at the root of their problems, even if they don't realize it in the beginning. The negative emotions are usually the underlying trigger for a wide range of other feelings that are often buried deep inside.

Sensation: We have five senses – sight, hearing, touch, taste, and smell, which contribute to all of our physiological experiences. Negative sensations may be butterflies in the stomach, tense muscles, physical pain, rapid heartbeat, headaches, cold hands or feet, sweating, nausea, skin crawling, and shortness of breath. Some more extreme sensations could also be hallucinations and/or illusions.

Imagery: This modality consists of the mental images that are built up in a person's mind. It includes things they may fantasize about, their daydreams, and their own personal self-image. Common in those who suffer from anxiety disorders, their fears are part of their imagery. They also have an excessive worry about the future. Those who struggle with depression may have images that are extremely negative and distorted, far from the reality of things. Addressing one's imagery will help them to learn how to adjust the view of the world and give them a more realistic and accurate view.

Cognition: Focuses on a person's beliefs, attitudes, and judgments. When thoughts are negative like limiting or distorted beliefs about something, they can contribute significantly to depression, anxiety, or any number of other disorders. When a person believes they are not worthy of something, it can have an impact on their relationships, employment, and other areas of their life, which can be very damaging.

Interpersonal Relationships: This takes a closer look at how they interact with others, their social skills, how they relate to people, and what kind of support system they have or is missing in their lives. A close look at their relationships will reveal if they know how to develop and maintain a lasting relationship, feel connected to others, and if they have a good balance in mental health. Those getting over a breakup, needing to resolve conflict, or are antisocial will usually find that they are also lacking in the areas of effect and cognition as well.

Drugs, Health, Biology: This is a combination of several things. First, it includes a person's physical health. Whether he has been fighting off any serious illnesses, his overall physical condition, any physical limitations, his age, or chronic pain are just some of the health concerns they may have. It will also include biological factors like his genetics and brain chemistry and his need for medical treatment or medications. Finally, this modality looks at his lifestyle habits including diet and nutrition, activity level, sleep and eating habits, smoking, and drug and alcohol use. Close attention needs to be considered when dealing with substances. Few people realize just how much of an impact these habits can have on your mood or mental state. By evaluating this factor carefully, you may be surprised at what it can reveal.

There are two ways these seven modalities can be assessed. It is either with a one-on-one interview with a therapist or by filling out a Multimodal Life History Inventory questionnaire. Once an assessment is determined based on the BASIC ID, then a program of therapeutic techniques and strategies can be implemented starting with the modality that represents the biggest problem.

Chapter 8: Rational Emotive Behavioral Therapy

Rational Emotive Behavioral Therapy (REBT) places most of its importance on the thought processes of an individual. Like all other forms of CBT, it is based on the same premise that what we think triggers our feelings, which in turn, will trigger our behavior. The main idea behind REBT is to help those people who view their personal experiences in a negative way. However, they do not address the experience directly. Instead, the behavior is adjusted based on how they "perceived" the experience.

Through REBT, patients are taught how to challenge their own beliefs and replace them with a more accurate line of reasoning. It targets the inner beliefs, so they can deal with their experiences in a more realistic way. When successful, it can be very powerful, changing not just the way one thinks but also their perception of life in general.

REBT works because it recognizes that logic is not always an effective part of the human psyche. Even with logic, it is not always the best way to solve problems. Computers operate entirely on logic to perform their functions; they absorb data, analyze it, and using logic determine an acceptable output. The human brain, however, processes information differently, often without the use of logic. Therefore, some of their conclusions can be far removed from reality.

The focus of Rational Emotive Therapy is to teach people to think in a more logical manner. It works to break down the instinctual thinking process by using logical reasoning to interfere with the irrational assumptions they are making. Once these irrational thoughts have been replaced with more positive ones, it will start to filter down and change the inappropriate behavior to actions that are more positive.

No matter what negative thought a person may have, its roots are often deep within an unrealistic world. To combat this type of reasoning, REBT applies something called the ABCDE model of thinking.

A: Activating Event

An inciting event is identified which triggers the irrational belief. This could be any number of negative experiences including an argument with someone, a car accident, or the loss of a job. It is the trauma of this event that compels the mind to create a new irrational thought or belief.

B: The Belief

Once the belief has been created, the mind will automatically revisit it every time a similar negative event occurs. Each time the mind goes back to the belief, it is reinforced causing the person to get stuck in a spiral of negative behavior without ever really understanding why it happened in the first place.

C: Consequences

The belief will trigger the consequences of their irrational thoughts. Some consequences could be emotional as in the case of guilt or shame, while others could be behavioral as in overeating or some form of substance abuse. The underlying emotions for these behaviors could be depression, lack of self-confidence, or hostility.

D: Dispute

The dispute phase of the program is when you learn to challenge that belief system and see it as irrational. You begin to recognize it as the root of your problems. At this stage, you learn to argue with your subconscious mind and dispute your negative beliefs. You will be asked to come up with convincing proof that will successfully contradict your imprinted way of thinking.

E: Effect

You could also call this phase reinforcement. Once you have had your internal debate and successfully convinced yourself that your irrational belief is wrong, more positive behaviors will be much easier to come by. You'll feel a stronger self-esteem, you'll be bolder, or you'll just feel a lot better overall.

In most cases, REBT can be done without the aid of a therapist. This model can help anyone get to the root of their negative behavior and arm them with the tools they need to change. It motivates people to look deeply at how their thoughts are developed and how to apply rationale to their beliefs and replace negative thoughts with a more realistic view that will build them up rather than tearing them down.

Chapter 9: Dialectical Behavior Therapy

Dialectical Behavior Therapy is more like a positive form of psychotherapy that can be tailored to treat those with some form of borderline personality disorder.

More like a form of "talk therapy," DBT focuses on the psychosocial elements of treatment. Its theory is based on the premise that some people's behavior is so extreme that their reaction to romantic, familial, or social relationships is a manner that is far removed from the norm.

Those who fall into this category experience emotional extremes where their arousal levels can happen very quickly and their emotions are at such a peak that the reactions are at a very high level, taking them much longer to return to normal after an episode. They generally see things only in black or white with extreme emotional outbursts that can leave quite a bit of damage in their wake.

Because of this, they find themselves falling into one problem after another with no internal ability to manage their emotions. Therefore, they get no relief when their emotions spiral out of control. DBT is made up of three different elements:

Support-Oriented: Identifying their strengths and learning how to use them to help them feel better about themselves.

Cognitive-Based: Identifying the negative thought patterns and finding new ways to cope with triggering events so that their lives are more stable.

Collaborative: Rooting out underlying problems by working through assignments, active role-play, and learning self-soothing practices, so they can manage their own outbursts.

Through each of these sessions, the focus will be on two primary components:

1. **Structured Individual Psychotherapy Sessions**

   Working with a therapist in a one-on-one session, patients will learn problem-solving behavior and openly discuss very specific issues that may have occurred in the past. These challenges could be anything from suicidal tendencies to self-mutilation. The more serious the issue, the more priority it should be given when working with the therapist. Minor issues may be assigned for the patient to deal with as homework.

During these sessions, you may also learn certain behaviors that can be applied to interrupt the negative habits. This adaptive behavior will have an emphasis on helping you to manage your emotions in the face of trauma much better. The objective here is to work towards a more socially acceptable behavior, so you can have better relationships with others.

2. **Group Therapy Sessions**

In group therapy, patients work their way through four different modules where they are taught practical skills they can rely on to help them cope with their negative patterns. Each skill has its own unique quality that can be used to minimize the negativity in their heads.

Mindfulness: A form of meditation where patients are helped to be more aware of their circumstances and the triggers that are causing their behaviors. Through mindfulness, they are taught how to observe, describe, and participate in their own thought processes as a neutral party. Then, with the use of special exercises, they learn how to recognize the triggers in their own mind, so they are better able to manage those reactions.

Interpersonal Effectiveness: Through practice sessions, they learn how to interact with others in a variety of scenarios. The process they go through is very similar to what is taught in many assertiveness training programs. Each session focuses on specific strategies to employ when getting to where they can ask for what they need, refuse things they don't, and specific coping mechanisms for when they are dealing with conflict.

Distress Tolerance: With distress tolerance, patients are given better ways to cope with disappointing and distressing circumstances. They learn how to accept things in a nonjudgmental manner. Rather than focusing on the negative, they will be better able to deal with real life situations that happen without their approval. Through this module, they are prepared with self-soothing techniques and other coping mechanisms that will reduce negative emotions and behavior.

Emotional Regulation: Learning how to regulate emotions is the key to managing negative behavior. Through the emotion regulation module, patients learn how to recognize the signs of oncoming intense emotions and use their coping strategies to manage them better. In this phase, they will be expected to address different emotional aspects including:

- Properly identifying and labeling their emotions when they arise.
- Recognizing the common obstacles that have been getting in the way of changing negative emotions.
- Lowering their susceptibility to negative emotions.
- Developing strategies to create more positive emotional experiences.
- Techniques that allow them to use their mindfulness to enhance positive emotions.
- They will also learn how to suppress their natural tendency long enough to choose another behavioral option opposite of what their instincts will do.
- They are given strategies they can utilize in distressful situations that will boost their tolerance levels.

With DBT, there are two main components, but because those that need CBT are most likely dealing with behavioral issues, they will focus most of their lessons in a group therapy environment, so they are able to practice their new skills and strategies they will need when interacting with others. DBT is still a relatively new program, but even so, it has already received recognition as a gold standard method of psychological treatment.

Conclusion

You began this book as someone who was unable to stop compulsive overeating and who was unsure of where to turn for support and advice. Now, you have found the solution to this problem and have learned everything you need to know about listening to. Your body, addressing your core wounds, and making healthier choices. This method has been proven to work for many, many people, and now that you are ready to put this into practice, you are going to find yourself in that category too.

The problem with emotional eating, or binge eating, and what makes it so difficult is that we need food in order to live, and we must eat multiple times a day, every day. This is unlike any other addiction where the person must stop drinking or using a drug altogether, as a person who is recovering from a food addiction must continue to eat.

If you have learned anything in this book, it is that you should allow yourself space to learn and grow and make mistakes. You should allow yourself to learn as you go and do not expect perfection right away. If you are dedicated to becoming an intuitive eater, you should allow yourself the time to practice. Just like any skill, you will need to practice and develop your skills of listening to your body and giving it what it needs.

As you begin your journey of intuitive eating, you will find that you develop a higher level of self-esteem, better feelings about your body image, and more optimism about life in general. Enjoy this journey of self-discovery, and don't forget to treat your body with the love and respect it deserves!

www.ingramcontent.com/pod-product-compliance
Lightning Source LLC
Chambersburg PA
CBHW071730080526
44588CB00013B/1977